TRUE VAMPIRES
OF HISTORY

TRUE VAMPIRES
OF HISTORY

by
DONALD F. GLUT

SENSE OF WONDER PRESS
James A. Rock & Company, Publishers
Rockville • Maryland

TRUE VAMPIRES OF HISTORY
by Donald F. Glut

SENSE OF WONDER PRESS
is an imprint of JAMES A. ROCK & CO., PUBLISHERS

Illustrations and photographs are from the collection of Forrest J Ackerman unless otherwise noted.

Front Cover Art: After a contemporary painting of the Roumanian ruler known as Vlad Ducla, Vlad Tepes, and Vlad "The Impaler" (1431-1476).

Back Cover: Still from the 1922 silent German film, *Nosferatu,* featuring Max Schreck in the eerie title role.

Frontispiece: An early woodcut of the original Count Dracula.

Address comments and inquiries to: SENSE OF WONDER PRESS
James A. Rock & Company, Publishers
9710 Traville Gateway Drive, #305
Rockville, MD 20850

E-mail:
jrock@rockpublishing.com   lrock@senseofwonderpress.com
Internet URL: www.SenseOfWonderPress.com

Paperbound ISBN: 0-918736-67-6
Hardbound ISBN: 0-918736-68-4

Printed in the United States of America

First Edition: December 2004

In Memory Of
Montague Summers

Contents

INTRODUCTION

The Evolution
of the Vampire Belief

by D. Scott Rogo

Through the ages the vampire and its tradition has been remodeled to fit the scientific and cultural developments of the era. The ancient Babylonians thought them to be evil demons, a view also entertained by the Greeks and Romans, though these two civilizations did acknowledge that the vampire could be the spirit of a once living and particularly evil person. With the advent of Christianity the vampire gained new proportions; it now became the spirit for of any person excommunicated by the Church. From this Christian concept of the vampire has come the elaborate folklore we now associate with it.

With the ever increasing scientific disposition of society, one might have felt that a belief in vampirism should have died off. Yet modern man once again only reinterpreted the phenomenon to maintain congruity with modern knowledge. When the "supernatural" was placed before critical eyes and scientific discrimination, with the founding of the Society for Psychical Research in 1882, the vampire still maintained his preeminence, and certain researchers promoted the theory that the vampire was a weird form of apparition that actually does thrive on some type of "life force." This apparitional view of the vampire fitted in quite neatly with the data the Society was collecting.

Turning through the annals of superstition, occultism, and psychism, we view many interesting and colorful people who have taken an interest in the vampire phenomenon.

The medieval occultists were the first to seriously contend that the vampire was a legitimate supernatural agency and a force with which to be reckoned. The Swiss alchemist, physician, scholar, and scientist, Paracelsus (Auroeleus Phillipus Theophrastus Paracelsus Bombast von Hohenheim) was one such character. Instead of condemning the vampire by Christian interpretations, Paracelsus actually was quite ahead of his time by theorizing that vampires were spirit entities and not the resurrected bodies of the dead. While a Renaissance figure (1491-1541), Paracelsus still clung to medieval metaphysics. And his occult writings, which included phenomenally acute descriptions of apparitions and poltergeists, show that even hundreds of years before the founding of the Society for Psychical Research occultists had not only accepted psychic phenomena as a scientific study, but had already categorized them and were conjecturing on their mechanism. It was Paracelsus who put forth the belief that the vampire was etheric, that they were spirits of the dead or elementals (spirits of the astral planes), and that perhaps the vampire was even an issuance from the soul and not actually the "astral body."

By the Eighteenth Century more "vampire hunters" had arisen. Perhaps unrecognized for his contributions, much of the present mythology of vampirism is due to the Austrian physician Dr. Johannes Von Loebl. During his vampire hunts in Serbia (1732), Von Loebl accepted the Roman Catholic authority of the vampire and believed that haematomaniacs during their earth life became vampires after death. It was he who prescribed the complicated process of destroying the vampire with which we are familiar today. Though his method did generously borrow from German customs, Von Loebl insisted on driving a stake through the suspected corpse. While only stating that the stake must be consecrated, this is a simplification of a process purportedly used in the Carpathian regions and in Eastern Europe wherein the stake must be made of pine wood and driven into the body with one blow piercing the heart. At this exact instant the head must also be severed by a sexton's spade; again only one blow is permitted. Von Loebl then ordered that the vampire's body must be burned, while the churchmen of the Middle Ages used the incineration of the body as an alternative to the stake. He also maintained that roses should be planted on the spot where the ashes of the creature were scattered. According to the German peasantry, a rose is placed on the coffin of the vampire. This paralyzes the monster until a pine stake can be made to formerly destroy it. Von Loebl did show that at least he was aware of the vampire heritage of his day. The use of the stake driven into the body has a long history and even today many primitive tribes in Africa drive a pike into every corpse before burial to insure against resurrection.

At about the same time Von Loebl was gadding about driving stakes into dead bodies, a much more sophisticated scholar was giving serious attention to tales of vampires. This was Dom Augustin Calmet, whose main treatise appeared in an English translation in 1759 as *Dissertation on Apparitions*. Later he added an appendix *Dissertation on Vampires*. While he too accepted the Church dictums on the demonic nature and physical properties of the vampire, his scholarly work was much more within the realms of physical research, for he does make mention of poltergeist phenomena and attributes them to the spirits of the dead. In a like manner he found it difficult to accept that vampires physically resurrect from their graves and could not comprehend how the vampire could enter and exit from a buried coffin. While he suggested that vampires are blood-sucking ghosts, his entire volume does show a total discomfort with vampirism as interpreted by the Church.

Calmet's predecessor Von Loebl noted that he could feel a slight pulse in vampire corpses and this ties in with another vampirologist Dr. Herbert Mayo. Mayo was firmly convinced that all superstitions had a foundation in fact, and in the years 1847-8 he wrote a series for *Blackwood's Edinburgh Magazine* entitled "On the Truths Contained in Popular Superstition." In these writings Mayo suggested defending the vampire as some sort of apparitional form. Obviously May was not familiar with the phenomenon of astral projection or he could have made an even more valuable contribution to our knowledge of vampirism.

It was not until the rise of spiritualism that vampirism took on a psychical denotation, even before the founding of the Society for Psychical Research. Throughout his scattered writings in the *Revue Spiritualiste*, Prof. Z.T. Pierart finally formed the view of vampirism that is complementary to psychical phenomena. His appraisal was that vampires are the actual result of astral projection coerced, as Mayo had suggested, by premature burial. This finally relegated the vampire enigma solely into the hands of a still scarce but growing scientific interest in psychic phenomena. Unfortunately Pierart's work was written before we knew much about astral projection, and they clearly hold a naive view of it. Written in 1858-78, they do not fall within the influence of the later French scientists who devoted much effort to fathoming the mystery of a psychic fluid—Lancelin, Durville, de Rochas, and others.

Perhaps the greatest of all the vampire hunters was Dr. Franz Hartmann. Though a great scholar on occultism and a firm believer in vampire phenomena, he never actually formulated a theory to explain them, though numerous theoretical points may be ascertained by reviewing his many articles on the subject.

Hartmann's life was as peculiar as his beliefs. While an Austrian, his travels included the United States where he was the proprietor of a gold mine. Later he became a theosophist and joined Helen Blavatsky, the founder of the Theosophical Society, and was her constant companion until her death shortly before 1900. In her old age Blavatsky was almost convinced by Hartmann to turn the presidency of the Theosophical Society over to him upon her death.

Before taking an interest in vampirism, Hartmann was an ardent spiritualist. The accounts of seances held in his home show him to have been fooled by the most puerile exhibitions of fraud imaginable. In Vienna he was a scholar on black magic with a special affinity for alchemy and even believed that an acquaintance of his had discovered the miracle of the philosopher's stone.

Hartmann's contribution to vampirology is double: his work as a scholar and as an active researcher. Many of his scholarly talents were put forth in his biography on Paracelsus which appeared in 1891. In this work Hartmann enunciates all the various entities that Paracelsus believed could induce vampirical attacks. Hartmann categorized them, explained them, and commented on them. There is no doubt that he fully accepted the belief that vampires are the astral forms of once living humans and postulates, as did Paracelsus, that suicides may turn into vampires, a belief already instituted by the Greek Orthodox Church.

Unlike Paracelsus, Calmet, and others, Hartmann was more than a scholar. He actively searched out actual instances of vampirism. Many of these cases were published in the *Occult Review* and *Border ½ line*, two occult journals edited by Ralph Shirley, also a noted psychist whose book on astral projection is one of the best in the field. In his articles such as "A Modem Case of Vampirism" and "An Authentic Vampire Story" Hartmann clearly defines his personal views of the phenomenon. Editorializing on the "Vampire Case of the Miller at D–" he discusses a new genre of vampire—a non-living, semiplastic force, that drains vitality from its victims, which he calls an "astral tumour." While never speculating to any degree on their nature, Hartmann does comment that he had run into the same genre many times previously. Hartmann elaborated on Paracelsus' theory of vampirism among the living and cited examples of this feature: cases where a fully conscious person unconsciously absorbs the vitality of others or willfully projects his astral body for the same purpose.

Two cohorts of Hartmann, who were themselves no amateurs in occultism, were Ralph Shirley and Bram Stoker. While we mostly associate Stoker with the novel *Dracula* he was, in fact, keenly interested in the phenomenon outside its journalistic possibilities and did travel to Hungary in order to thoroughly research the vampire legend among the superstitious peasantry. Oddly when *Dracula* appeared in 1897 it was re- published by Ralph Shirley who was then president of Rider Co., the famous English publishing house. He was, as mentioned, editor of two occult journals and had already written several of his many books on psychical research and related fields. Here we see an interesting parallel between the work of the publisher Shirley, the investigator Hartmann, and the writer Stoker. Hartmann would often conduct seances in order to contact the vampire spirit. The hair-raising account of a vampire- haunted castle in the Hartz Mountains is one of the best documented vampire cases from Hartmann's files. Toward the end of *Dracula* Mina Harker, having become the victim of the King Vampire, becomes a trance medium through whom Count Dracula's pursuers discover his whereabouts, chase him back to his homeland and destroy him. This is much the same method Hartmann claimed to have used in employing professional mediums. In fact the vampire expert in Stoker's novel, Dr. Van Helsing, is a caricature of Dr. Franz Hartmann, even the names being similar. Ralph Shirley stated as late as 1924 that "It may be doubted indeed, in spite of the lack of records, whether vampirism in one form or another, is quite as absent from the conditions of modern civilization as is commonly supposed."

While by the turn of the century a belief in the blood-sucking vampire had somewhat disappeared, random reports still flowed into Occult journals: the Croglin Grange vampire, Breene's report of one to the *Occult Review* in 1925, and even Hartmann acknowledged one in 1895.

While it appears that by the turn of the century and the founding of the Society for Psychical Research a degree of sophistication had been reached concerning an understanding of vampirism, the Roman Catholic Church and its demonist theory was still quite alive. By 1930 two books appeared that again re-evaluated and supported the Church view of vampirism, *The Vampire: His Kith and Kin* and *The Vampire in Europe*. Both of these volumes were by the witchcraft scholar Montague

Summers who, like his historical colleagues, led a curious and mysterious life. Although an ordained minister of the Church of England, he converted to Roman Catholicism shortly after his ordination and thereafter devoted himself to an historical study of witchcraft. For long periods of time he seemed to have disappeared. The only person to know his residency for these protracted periods was his secretary, who ominously died shortly after Summers. In the latter of his two volumes Summers puts to his readers his personal convictions on the nature of vampirism. These are interesting as Summers seems to be authoritively speaking from the Catholic viewpoint.

Summers was more intrigued by the blood-sucking belief than the scientific considerations of his day and felt the vampire to be inherently evil and a device of Satan. Summers stated that the actual mechanics of the vampire are unknown but they are not self-animated. He falls back on the ancient belief that vampires are zombies animated by an evil spirit. This spirit is, of course, a direct emissary from Satan and the suitability 'of the corpse is due to a hidden faculty (sic) of the body not yet understood. He also disagreed with the popular custom of warding off vampires by the use of amulets, but gives no alternate method.

Meanwhile occultists were also beginning to believe that the vampire was more than just a freak of the death experience.

Many modern occultists agreed with the Roman Catholic Church that perhaps the vampire was inherently evil, but still maintained that it was an etheric, not physical, being. Such modern occultists as Eliphas Levi (Abbe Gonstant), Dion Fortune, and C. W. Leadbeter felt that the astral body could sustain itself on the earth plane and keep itself from evolving into the higher worlds by certain occult practices.

Certain of their theories are quite attractive and even Montague Summers' out of date references and commentaries are carefully thought out. They quote Hartmann and prominent psychic literature of the day, which is more than many occultists did.

Perhaps the last of the vampire hunters was the psychoanalyst Nandor Fodor. Fodor encountered a vampire case with Mrs. Forbes, the center of a poltergeist attack. While never actually believing it to be more than the morbid fantasy of a diseased mind, he does devote a chapter of his book *On the Trail of the Poltergeist* to the subject.

There is no doubt that Mrs. Forbes was a mentally sick woman. But there has always been a direct relationship between vampire attacks and poltergeist attacks. Even Calmet made note of this. And there are cases of "biting poltergeists." It is only fair to note that Mrs. Forbes' husband also felt the presence of an unseen force and after the attacks began she started an episode of trance mediumship reminiscent of Hartmann. Fodor reveals that the woman was not aware of Stoker's novel by the use of various psychological tests. The case is dated 1938.

In Fodor's posthumously published book *Between Two Worlds* he cites and apparently accepts an instance of vampirism.

The vampire has lent itself to many interpretations—as a zombie, a ghoul, and as an astral projection. With the development of psychical science has come new considerations of supposed superstitions and so has developed a new understanding of the vampire—but one supported by fact.

D. Scott Rogo is a parapsychologist who has written several papers on vampire beliefs and traditions. He has published a book and several articles on parapsychology in such periodicals as the *International Journal of Parapsychology* and *The Parapsychology Review*.

AUTHOR'S INTRODUCTION
True Vampires of History

This book is not fiction.

Surely that is an incredible statement to make introducing a book about vampires or the undead. Twentieth Century persons living in an age of technology cannot really believe in the existence of the resuscitated corpse, with elongated canine fangs contrasted against chalky complexion, leaving the grave to suck the blood of living victims. Or can they?

Belief in vampires has persisted from the days of ancient Greece and Rome through the present. As a descendant of generations of Croatians, Hungarians, Austrians, and Germans, I have heard many tales of people barring their doors and hanging garlic and crosses over their beds to prevent a visitation by one of these living dead.

The amount of evidence asserting the existence of the undead is staggering. These accounts are not to be merely laughed away as the products of superstition and hysteria. Cases of vampirism—in the supernatural sense—are too numerous, fully documented and witnessed by such reputable observers as priests, doctors, military officers, and scholars, to be disregarded as sheer myth.

This book does not intend to prove the existence of vampires; nor is it to categorize the traits of the undead. It is merely an assemblage of cases of vampirism arranged in chronological order.

—DONALD F. GLUT

Vampire Emperor of Rome

Gaius Julius Caesar Germanicus, popularly known as "Caligula," was assassinated by a vengeful Praetorian guard on 24 June 41. The wicked Roman Emperor had insulted the guard, only to lay dead at his feet. Although Caligula was dead his evil lingered. There existed the dread possibility that Emperor Caligula would return from the grave as a vampire.

The writer Suetonius recorded the precautions taken to end the threat of the vampire:

"His body was carried privately into the Lamian Gardens, where it was half burned upon a pyre hastily raised and then had a small quantity of earth carelessly thrown over it. It was afterwards disinterred by his sisters upon their return from banishment; it was decorously cremated and the ashes buried. Yet before this was done, it was very well known that the keepers of the Gardens were greatly disturbed by horrid apparitions, and not a night passed without some terrible alarm or other, whilst the house in which he had been murdered was suddenly burned to the ground."

A belief existed in Ancient Rome that the spirit of an exceptionally evil man continued to lurk about his tomb after death. For Caligula to be stopped before he could begin a career as a vampire, his body required cremation, a method of vampire destruction later commonplace among the Slavs, English, Greeks, and others. The Lamian Gardens were located on Mount Esquiline, an oak covered mound stained by the blood of human sacrifice. The hill had a long history of death and haunting.

Caligula, born on 31 August 12 of Germanicus, the adopted son and nephew of Tiberius Caesar and Agrippina Major, was so nicknamed because of the "Little Boots" he wore as a child when accompanying his father into military campaigns. When his father died, Caligula lived with his mother until she was arrested for her involvement in a conspiracy in the year 29. Caligula later joined Emperor Tiberius on the isle of Capri. In the year 33 he and the Emperor's grandson were made joint heirs to Tiberius' estate. But when Tiberius died in 37 the Roman

Senate declared the will invalid, leaving Caligula the sole heir. Gamellus was soon to become the adopted son of Caligula, who was now Emperor of Rome.

The first year of Caligula's reign was relatively peaceful and prosperous. He was a handsome, well educated man, quite popular with his subjects. Caligula's impressionable mind gradually degenerated with power until he could not control his own sense of greatness. He became a cruel despot, answering his enemies by shedding their blood. Descended from Julius Caesar, Caligula believed himself divine and demanded the public worship him. He attempted to deify his deceased sister Drusilla and built a bridge that joined his palace on the Palatine to the Capitoline Hill, so that he might more easily have conferences with Jupiter at his temple. The ruler of Rome went so far as to demand a statue of himself be erected inside the Temple of Jerusalem, a task interrupted by his death. Before he died the Emperor spilled much Jewish blood.

Within a year he squandered all of his fortune, much of it going to his favorite horse Incitatus, which received a marble stable, an ivory stall, and a jeweled collar. Rumors hinted that Caligula was considering making a consul of the beast.

The man was despised and at least two unsuccessful conspiracies were launched against him; one involving his sisters Livilla and Agrippina, the other with Gaetulicus, legate of Upper Germany. Both conspiracies were discovered and smashed.

Accomplishing virtually nothing during his bloody reign, Caligula, the most monstrous emperor of them all, died a raving madman, hated and feared in death as well as in life.

VAMPIRES DESCRIBED BY WALTER MAP

Vampirism was strongest in England during the Twelfth Century. In Walter Map's *De Nugis Curialium*, his treatise on the Middle Ages (dated between 1181 and 1193 by Dr. James) we find several accounts of English vampires.

One night during the reign of William the Conqueror, Eric Wilde of the manor of North Ledbury was staying near an old abandoned inn. Peeking out of his window he observed a number of gorgeous women who reminded him of tales "of the wanderings of spirits and how troops of demons appear at night, and to see them is death, and Dictinna (who is identified with Diana) and bands of Dryads and Vampires."

An old decree mentioned "some wicked women,. wholly given over to Satan and caught the illusions and glamours of demons, believe and profess that they ride abroad at night with Diana on certain feasts, accompanied by an innumerable host of women, passing over immense distances, obeying her commands as their mistress, and evoked by her upon certain nights."

As Lord Eric Wilde peered from his window he wondered if this group of women were a company of vampires.

Another case of vampirism was related by Map as the story of a knight and his deceased wife. Having been already buried, the wife returned to "life" when the knight rescued her from a band of fairy dancers. In her resuscitated condition she became the mother of many children, called in their number the "Sons of the dead woman."

An excellent history of a vampire is recounted in Map's Second Division, Chapter Fourteen. A knight, having wed a serious, religious society woman, was aghast at a horrible incident on the morning following the birth of his first child. The baby's throat had been slit so that blood stained the cradle. A second child was born a year later, then a third. The same horrible thing happened despite the watchings of the knight and the rest of the household. When his wife again announced her pregnancy, she and the knight tried to sway the wrath of God through prayer and sacrifice.

The house and the surrounding area were brightly illuminated when the fourth child was born This time, they resolved, nothing would enter of a malevolent nature that would escape their notice and vengeance.

It was then that a stranger, tired from his long journey, begged entrance to the house in the name of God. The knight admitted him and told the sad reasons of their vigil. Sympathizing and grateful for their hospitality, the stranger offered to stay up and await the unknown killer of children.

Midnight found the members of the household mysteriously falling asleep. The stranger, shocked and bewildered, managed to resist the compulsion to sleep. Through his heavy eyes he saw the trusted matron bend over the cradle. She was about to slit the child's throat. Without hesitation the stranger sprang forward and seized the woman, resulting in such a commotion that everyone awakened and identified the captured murderess. To their astonishment it was the most trusted and loved matron in the city.

The matron was questioned. But she refused to give her name or any other information. The knight, believing that she was merely too ashamed to speak, let her go. The stranger, however replied that she was a diabolical vampire. He pressed a key to the nearby church against her face, branding her with its holy impression.

The knight asked how such a well known woman could have been a demon undetected for so many years. The stranger replied that she was not a woman but a monster in disguise. He sent some members of the household to fetch the real woman whom the vampire resembled. The true matron then looked at her double bewildered. Across the face of the matron was a mark identical to the key brand on the vampire's scowling face.

The stranger then remarked, "There can be no doubt that the lady who has now come is very virtuous and very dear to heaven, and that by her good works she has stiffed hell and provoked the anger of devils against her, and so this evil messenger of theirs, this loathsome instrument of their wrath has been fashioned as far as possible in the likeness of this noble lady, that this demon may cause this noble soul to be accused of the guilt for her heinous deeds. And in order that you may believe, see what she will do after I release her."

The vampire stood away from the others. Then howling and screeching like an animal she flew away from the window and, defeated, never returned to the house again.

This case in which a good woman was impersonated by a vampiric entity was further explained by an example reported by Fathers Kramer and Sprenger in the *Malleus Maleficarum*, Part II, Question 1, XI.

"The injury to reputation is shown in the history of the Blessed Jerome, that the devil transformed himself into the appearance of S. Silvanus, Bishop of Nazareth, a friend of S. Jerome. And this devil approached a noble woman by night in her bed and began first to provoke and entice her with lewd words, and then invited her to perform the sinful act. And when she called out, the devil in the form of the saintly Bishop hid under the woman's bed, and being sought for and found there, he in lickerish language, declared lyingly that he was the Bishop of Silvanus. On the morrow, therefore, when the devil. had disappeared, the holy man was heavily defamed; but his good name was cleared when the devil confessed at the tomb of S. Jerome that he had done this in an assumed body."

Map continued his accounts of vampires with the following history.

"The most wonderful thing that I know of happened in Whales. William Laudun, an English soldier, a man of great strength and proven courage, went to Gilbert Foliot, who was at that time Bishop of Hereford, but is now Bishop of London, and said to him, 'My lord, I come to thee to ask for counsel. A certain Welsh malefactor recently died in my house, a man professed to believe in nothing, and after an interval of four nights he has returned each night and has not failed on each occasion to summon forth severally and by name one of his fellow lodgers. As soon as they are called by him they sicken and within three days they die, so that now but a few are laft.' The Bishop, who was greatly amazed, answered: 'Perhaps power hath been given by the Lord to the evil angel of that accursed wretch so that he is able to rouse himself and walk abroad in his dead body. However, let the corpse be exhumed, and then do you cut through its neck sprinkling both the body and grave throughout with holy water, and so rebury it.' This was accordingly done, but none the less the survivors were tormented and attacked by the wandering spirit. Now it happened that on a certain night when only very few were left William himself was called three times by name. But he being bold and active and knowing who it was suddenly rushed out, brandishing his drawn sword. The demon fled fast but he pursued it to the very grave, and as it lay therein he clave its head through from the neck. At that very hour, the persecution they endured from this demonical wanderer ceased, and since that time neither William himself nor any one of the others has suffered any harm therefrom. We know that this thing is true, but the cause of the haunting remains unexplained."

In Chapter xxviii Map related:

"*Another Marvel.* We also know that in the time of Roger, Bishop of Worcester, a certain man who, as it was commonly bruited, died an atheist in his sins, wandered about and was encountered by many who saw him, dressed in a hair-shirt, until he was surrounded in an orchard by all the people of the neighbourhood. And it was stated that he was seen there for three days. We know, moreover, that this same Bishop Roger ordered that a cross should be erected over the grave of the unhappy wretch and that the spirit should be laid. But when the demon had come to the grave, and a great crowd of people followed him, he leaped back in alarm—as we think, at the sight of the cross and he fled elsewhere. Then the people, acting upon wise advice, removed the cross, and the demon rushed into the grave covering himself with earth, and immediately after the cross was raised upon it again so that he was lain there without causing any disturbance."

Vampirism mysteriously subsided as an English belief following the Twelfth Century, until its revival in the 1800s.

THE VAMPIRE HUSBAND

William of Newburgh related various accounts of vampires in England in Book V of his Chronicles (1196). The events took place during the reign of King Richard I:

"Chapter xxii: *Of the extraordinary happening when a dead man wandered abroad out of his grave.*

"About that time in the county of Buckinghamshire a most remarkable event took place, and this I first heard of from some people who lived in that very district, and it was afterwards told me in fullest detail by Stephen, the highly respected and most worthily esteemed Archdeacon of that diocese. A certain man having died, according to the course of nature, was by the seemly care of his wife and relations decently buried on the Eve of Ascension Day (29th May). But on the following night he suddenly entered the room where his wife lay asleep and, having awakened her, he not only filled her with the greatest alarm but almost killed her by leaping upon her with the whole heaviness of his weight and overlying her. On the second night, also, he tormented the trembling woman in just the same way. Wherefore in the extremity of dread she resolved that on the third night she would remain awake and that then and thenceforth she would protect herself from this horrible attack by providing a company of persons to watch with her. Nevertheless, he visited her; but when he was driven away by the shouts and cries of those who were keeping watch, so that he found he could do her no harm, he swiftly departed. Having been thus baffled and repulsed by his wife, he proceeded in exactly the same manner to harass and annoy his brothers who resided in the same town. But they, taking pattern from the excellent precautions employed by their sister-in-law, passed several nights of wakefulness, surrounded by their household all on guard, and all ready to receive and repel the onset of the dead man. He made his appearance, indeed, but it seemed as though he were only wishful, or only had the power, to molest those who were asleep, and he was kept at bay by the vigilance and the courage of any who were on their guard and waking. Next, then, he roved about and beset animals

Max Schreck in the eerie 1922 silent German film, "Nosferatu."

who were either in the houses or resting near the houses. This was
discovered by the unusual panic and disturbances of the terrified beasts.
So eventually since he proved so terrible and continual a danger both
to friends and neighbours alike, there was nothing for it save that they
should pass their nights in watching and being continually on their
guard. Accordingly throughout the town in every house there were certain of the family who kept awake and mounted guard all night long,
whilst everybody was anxious and fearful lest they should be subjected
to some sudden and unforeseen attack. Now when for a good while he
had harried people during the night alone, he began to wander abroad
in plain daylight, dreaded by all, although actually he was seen but by a
few. Very often he would encounter a company of some half-a-dozen
and he would be quite clearly discerned by but one or two of the number, although all of them very perceptibly felt his horrible presence.
Wellnigh scared out of their senses the inhabitants at last determined
that they must seek counsel from the church; and accordingly with
many piteous lamentations, they laid the whole matter from first to last
before Archdeacon Stephen, whom I have mentioned above, in his public and official capacity as president of a diocesan synod which was
then convened. The Archdeacon forthwith wrote a letter to that vener-
able prelate, His Lordship the Bishop of Lincoln (S. Hugh), who happened to be at London. The screed related all these extraordinary circumstances in regular order, and he requested his lordship to give directions as to what must be done to remedy so intolerable an evil, since
he felt that the matter should be dealt with by the. highest authority.
When the Bishop heard of this he was greatly amazed, and forthwith he
consulted with a number of learned priests and reverend theologians,
from certain of whom he learned that similar occurrences had often
taken place in England, and many well-known instances were quoted to
him. They all agreed that the neighbourhood would never obtain any
peace until the body of that miserable wretch had been disinterred and
burned to ashes. However, such a method seemed extremely undesir-
able and unbecoming to the holy Bishop, who forthwith wrote out
with his own hand a chartula of absolution and sent this to the Archdeacon ordaining that, whatever might be the reason why the man wandered about his grave, the tomb should be opened, and when the chartula
of absolution had been laid upon the breast of the corpse, all should
once again be fastened up as before. Therefore they opened the tomb,
and the body was found therein uncorrupt, just as it had been laid

upon the day of his burial. The chartula of Episcopal absolution was placed upon his breast, and after the grave had again been closed, the dead man never wandered abroad, nor had he the power to injure or frighten anybody from that very hour."

CONCERNING
THE BERWICK VAMPIRE

In Book V of William of Newburgh's *Chronicles* we find the following vampire account:

"Chapter xxiii. *Concerning a similar occurrence which happened at Berwick.* It has come to our knowledge that about the same time a similar and no less great wonder took place in the extreme north of England. There is a fine and flourishing town at the mouth of the river Tweed, called Berwick, which comes under the jurisdiction of the King of Scotland. Here then dwelt a certain man who was indeed surpassing rich in this world's goods, but, as later only too clearly came to light, a most infamous villain. Now, after he was buried, at night he used by the power of Satan, as we may very well believe, continually to issue forth from his grave, and to rush up and down the streets of the town, whilst the dogs howled and bayed in every direction what time this evil thing was abroad. Any citizen who chanced to meet him was distraught with terror, and then just before daybreak he returned to his grave. When this had been going on for some little time nobody dared to step outside his door after nightfall, so terribly did they all dread to meet this fatal monster. Accordingly the authorities, as well as men of poor estate, earnestly discussed what steps had best be taken to rid themselves of so sore a visitation, for even the most thoughtless and irresponsible of them were extremely apprehensive lest, if by some unlucky chance they met this living corpse, they would be fearfully assaulted and injured by the dead man; whilst those who were more sagacious and far-sighted were afraid lest, unless some speedy remedy were found, owing to the fact that black decomposition of this foul body horribly infected the air with poisonous pollution as it rushed to and fro, the plague or another fatal disease might break out and sweep away many, a disaster which had not infrequently been known to happen in circumstances similar to this. Accordingly they chose among them ten young men of singular bravery and strength and bade them exhume this accursed corpse. It was then to be hewn member from member and cut into small pieces, and thrown into a blazing furnace so that it might be entirely burned up and consumed. When this had been done the prevailing panic was calmed, 'and the slaughter ceased' (Psalm cv. 30). For the monster, while he was roving abroad by the power of Satan as we have explained, is said to have announced to certain persons whom he encountered that the people should have no rest until his body were consumed to ashes. Therefore, when he had been burned it seemed in truth as though the people had a certain period of rest, but there very shortly broke out a terrible pestilence which carried off the greater part of that town. And nowhere else did the plague rage so fiercely, although, certes about the same time there was an epidemic in several districts of England."

VAMPIRES OF MELROSE ABBEY AND ALNWICK CASTLE

William of Newburgh concluded his narrative with the following text:

"Chapter xxiv. *Concerning certain marvelous events.* It is, I am very well aware, quite true that unless they were amply supported by many examples which have taken place in our own days, and by the unimpeachable testimony of responsible persons, these facts would not easily be believed, —to wit, that the bodies of the dead may arise from their tombs and that vitalized by some supernatural power, they speed hither and thither, either greatly alarming or in some cases actually slaying the living, and when they return to the grave it seems to open to them of its own accord. It does not appear that any similar occurrences took place in ancient times, since nothing of the sort is found in old histories, and we know that those writers were always eager to include in their chapters any extraordinary or wonderful event. For we cannot suppose that, inasmuch as they never hesitated to discourse at length about any unusual happening, if circumstances such as these, which are not only most horrible but also most surprising, had taken place in their days they would have been able to refrain from treating them in detail. And yet if I were to set down all the stories of this kind which, as I have ascertained, have taken place in our day, my chronicle would not be merely extremely prolific and diffuse but, I suspect, it would become not a little. wearisome to read. Accordingly, in addition to those I have mentioned above, I will only give examples of two quite recent occurrences, and since the opportunity offers, it will, I make no doubt, be profitable to relate these in the course of our history, for they may well serve as a timely warning to my readers.

"Some years ago there died the chaplain of a certain lady of high rank, and he was buried in that stately and magnificent monastery, the Abbey of Melrose. Unfortunately, this priest little respected the sacred vows of his holy order and he passed his days almost as if he were a layman. In particular was he devoted to that idle sport than which scarcely any vanity so cheapens the character and harms the reputation of a priest, whose business it is to minister the Holy Sacraments of the Church, to wit, hunting with horse and hounds, for which he was so notorious that by many he was mockingly nicknamed Hundeprest, that is Dog Priest. And it was quite plain from what happened after his death that he was commonly held in very light esteem, and his guilt was almost censurable, nay, even heinous. For several nights he made his way out of his grave and endeavored to force an entrance into the cloister itself, but herein he failed and he was unable either to injure or even alarm anybody at all, so great were the merits and the holiness of the good monks who lived there. After that he preceeded to wander further abroad, and suddenly appeared in the chamber at the very bedside of the lady whose chaplain he had been and uttered the most piercing shrieks and heartrending groans. When this had taken place more than once, she was almost distraught with fear, dreading that some terrible danger might happen to her, and summoning a senior in the brethren from the monastery she besought him with tears that they should offer special prayers on her behalf since she was tormented in a most extraordinary and unusual manner. When he had heard her story the monk calmed her anxiety, for by her frequent benefactions and charities she had deserved well of Melrose and of all the brethren, and sympathizing with her in her misfortune, he promised that before long a remedy should be found. As soon as he had returned to the monastery he divulged his plan to a prudent and wise monk, and they decided that in company with two stout and brave-hearted young men, they would watch all night in that part of the graveyard where the unhappy priest had been buried. These four, therefore, armed with spiritual as well as earthly weapons and secured by their companionship, proceeded to pass the whole night on the spot. Accordingly, three of the company withdrew for a while that they might warm themselves by the fire in a lodge near at hand, for the night air nipped sharp and bitter cold, yet the monk who had requested the others to join him resolved not to relinquish his vigil. Now when he was left alone in the place, the Devil, thinking that he had found a fine opportunity to break down the pious man's courage and constancy, aroused from his grave that instrument of his which apparently he had once allowed to slumber a longer time than usual. When the monk saw the monster close at hand, realizing that he was all alone, he felt a thrill of horror; but in a moment his courage returned. He had no thought of flight, and as the horrible creature rushed at him with the most hideous yell, he firmly stood his ground, dealing it a terrible blow with a battle-axe which he held in his hand. When the dead man received this wound he groaned aloud with a terrible hollow noise, and swiftly turning he fled away no less quickly than he had appeared. But this brave monk followed hard on his heels as he escaped, and compelled him to seek refuge in his grave. This seemed promptly to open to him of its own accord, and when it had sheltered its inmate from his pursuer, it quickly closed over him, the ground appearing undisturbed. Whilst this was going on the three who, shivering from the chill and damps of night, had gone off to warm themselves at the fireside, came running up, a few minutes too late, however to see what had taken place. However, when they heard the whole story, they at once decided that at the first break of day they must disinter this accursed corpse and no longer suffer it to remain buried in their churchyard. When they had cleared away the earth and the corpse to light they found it marked by a terrible wound, whilst the black blood that had flowed from this seemed to swamp the whole tomb. The carrion, therefore, was carried to a remote place outside the bounds of the monastery, where it was burned in a huge fire and the ashes scattered to the winds. I have related this story quite simply and in a straightforward manner just as it was told to me by the monks themselves.

"Another history of the same kind but even more terrible and more fatal, happened in connection with Alnwick Castle, and this I learned from a very devout old priest of high authority and most honourable reputation, who dwelt in that district, and who informed me that he had actually been a witness of these terrible happenings. A certain man of depraved and dishonest life, either through fear of the law, or else shunning the vengeance of his enemies, left the country of Yorkshire, where he was living and betaking himself to the said castle, whose lord he had long known, settled down there. Here he busied himself in lewd traffic, and he seemed rather to persevere in his wickedness than to endeavor to correct his ways. He married a wife and this soothly proved his bane, as afterwards was clearly shown. For on a day when wanton stories were whispered in his ear concerning his spouse, he was fired with a raging jealousy. Restless and full of anxiety to know whether the charges were true, he pretended that he was going on a long journey and would not return for several days. He stole back, however, that very evening, and was secretly admitted into his wife's bedchamber by a serving wench who was privy to his design. Here he crept quietly up and lay at length upon the rooftwig which ran just over the bed, so that he might see with his own eyes if she violated her nuptial faith. Now when he espied there beneath him his wife being well served by a lusty youth, a near neighbour, in his bitter wrath he clean forgot his perilous position, and in a trice he had tumbled down, falling heavily to the ground just at the side of the bed where the twain were clipping at clicket. The young cuckold-maker beat a hasty retreat; but his wife, very cunningly concealing her avouterie, hastened to raise him gently from the floor. Anon he comes to himself, and rails at her as a common whore, threatening a speedy punishment. 'Ah, my dear,' replied the lady, 'sign yourself, I pray you, for you are talking wildly; you rail, and yet this is the result of your lusts, no doubt, for you know not what to say.' Now he was indeed exceedingly shaked from the fall, and being sore and bruised and most painfully benumbed over his whole body he became exceedingly ill. The good priest who related this story to me, visited him out of charity and for duty's sake, warning him that he should make a full confession of all his sins, and receive the Blessed Sacrament as Christians use. But he, in answer, related what had happened to him, together with the crafty words of his wife, and he put off fulfilling the timely and pious admonition until the morrow, but on the morrow he was dead. For during that very night this wretched man, who was so great a stranger to God's grace and whose crimes were so many, sank into the sleep of death. And yet, all unworthy as he was, they gave him a Christian burial, which he did not deserve and which profited him nothing. For by the power of Satan in the dark hours he was wont to come forth from his tomb and to wander about all through the streets, prowling round the houses, whilst on every side the dogs were howling and yelping the whole night long. Throughout the whole district then every man locked and barred his door, nor did anyone between the hours of dusk and dawn fare to go out on any business whatsoever, so greatly did each one fear that he might haply meet this fell monster and be attacked and most grievously harmed. Yet even these precautions were of no avail. For the air became foul and tainted as this fetid and corrupting body wandered abroad, so that a terrible plague broke out and there was hardly a house which did not mourn its dead, and presently the town, which but a little while before had been thickly populated, seemed to be wellnigh deserted, for those who had survived the pestilence and these hideous attacks hastily removed themselves to other districts lest they also should perish. The parish priest, the good man from whom I learned this story, was grieved to the heart at this trouble which had fallen upon his flock and at the desolation of his cure. Accordingly upon Palm Sunday he called together a number of wise and devout men who might advise him what best course to take in such perilous circumstances, and who might at least console the few wretched souls yet remaining even if it were with no very high hopes of affording them relief. There ceremonies of the day, therefore, were carried out with special solemnity, and after he had made a sermon to the people, the good priest invited to his table the devout religious whom he had summoned, together with a number of leading citizens and other honourable men. Whilst they were sat at meat, two young men, brothers, who had lost their father in the recent pestilence, reasoned with one another, thus: "This monster hath slain our father, and if we do not look about he will before long slay us too. Let us, therefore, dare a bold deed which will both provide for our own safety and also avenge the murder of our dear father. There is no one to hinder us, for the chief men of the district are set at meat in the presbytery, and throughout the whole town there is a silence as if it were altogether forsaken and dead. Let us, therefore, exhume this foul pest and let us burn him to ashes with fire." They armed themselves, therefore with sharp spades and betaking themselves to the cemetery, they began to dig. And whilst they yet thought they would have to dig much deeper, suddenly they came upon the body, covered with but a thin layer of earth. It was gorged and swollen with a frightful corpulence, and its face was florrid and chubby, with huge, red puffed cheeks, and the shroud in which it had been wrapped was all soiled and torn But the young men, who were mad with grief and anger, were not in any way frightened. They at once dealt the corpse a sharp blow with the keen edge of the spade, and immediately there gushed out such a stream of warm red gore that they realized this vampire (*sanguisuga*) had battened in the blood of many poor folk. Accordingly they dragged it outside the town, and here they quickly built a large pyre. When this was in a blaze, they went to the priest's house and informed the assembled company what they had done. There was not a man of these who did not hasten to the spot, and who was not a witness, if future testimony were required, of what had taken place. Now, no sooner had that infernal monster been thus destroyed than the plague, which had so sorely ravaged the people, entirely ceased, just as if the polluted air was cleansed by the fire which burned up the hellish brute."Vampires and the Black DeathCases of vampiric attacks on the living were often reported when the Black Death swept across Tyrol. Marienberg, a Benedictine abbey, was touched severely by the plague. The abbey was also said to have been favorite target of vampires. One of the monsters' victims was a monk Dom Steino von Netten. The incident was recorded by Sebastian Moelers in 1343.

DRACULA

The most universally known vampire of all is unquestionably Count Dracula. The character has been immortalized in various media, especially the novel *Dracula* by Bram Stoker, first published in 1897, and in numerous motion pictures starring such actors as Bela Lugosi, John Carradine, and Christopher Lee. The name "Dracula" is indeed a household word. However, few people realize that Dracula is in fact an his *historical* figure who *drank human blood*.

The actual Dracula was the subject of a very accurate history by Count Feodor Kuritsinn around the year 1482; in a semi-fictionalized book *The Great Monster* by German historian Michale Beheim in 1491; and in an epic of three volumes titled *Voivoda Dracula* by the Rumanian writer Mihai Sadovianu in the Sixteenth Century.

It was upon this historical Dracula that Bram Stoker based his novel of the notorious vampire count. Stoker cited in his novel certain "Arminius" who was actually Arminius Vambery of Budapest, who supplied him with such information concerning the Dracula who was referred to as "The Impaler." Stoker incorporated what he learned of this historical Dracula in telling the origins of his romanticized character.

Hungary was a strong nation in 1431 with territorial powers extending to Wallachia (or Valachia), which is now Romania. That particular area was ruled by a certain Vlad, raised to the title of Voivode or Prince by King Sigismund of Hungary. The King (later the Holy Roman. Emperor) had founded an exclusive society of uniformed knights, the Order of the Dragon. As a bonus to Vlad he was made a member of the Order. His subjects traditionally associated *dragon* with *devil* and began to whisper that their Voivode was in league with Satan. The man's cruel acts were widely known and did not subtract the suspicions.

Wallachia was invaded by the Turks in 1455. The result was that Vlad IV, the Voivode's son, became their puppet ruler. It was this fourth Vlad that came to be known as Dracula, the human vampire.

Vlad IV was a traitor, betraying the Christians to the Turks to further his pursuits after wealth and power. In return he was given control of the Ciglesz Castle over which flew his own crest of black and red. The castle became a veritable prison wherein were held a large number of Christian captives. The Voivode was to, collect their ransom for the Turks from a band of French emissaries. The Frenchmen's honor proved their bane. They were willing to pay the commanded price for the prisoners. But they would not take off their hats to a man with an assumed title, especially one given by the enemy. Vlad they considered no more than a lowly thief. The Voivode's eyes blazed. Immediately he had the insolent Frenchmen bound to stakes. Then he personally nailed their hats to their heads. If they managed to survive the torture their leg arteries were slashed and the blood caught in basins. For the next three days the Voivode bathed in the collected human blood.

During the next year Vlad commended that on a prescribed day all cripples, beggars, widows, orphans, and senior citizens without living relatives congregate in his castle. After being treated to a hearty meal each person was told to enter a certain room where they would be given a new set of clothes and an ample monetary gift. The people should have suspected their monarch's sudden generosity. For as each hardship case entered that room he was attacked by Vlad's cutthroats and maced or piked to death. The wolves and bears in Vlad's private zoo feasted well that day.

Vlad wrote of himself, "I bequeath to thee my kingdom without any beggars, orphans or cripples whom I have spared further suffering in this world."

On another occasion he claimed to be responsible for the production of many saints by sending large numbers of human souls into heaven. He sounded like Caligula. Most distressing was Vlad's belief in his own words.

Shortly Vlad was referred to by a number of names, all stemming from the Latin root *draco* for *devil* or *dragon*. The name *Dracula* became commonplace; Venice called him *Dragulia*; Germany knew him as *Dracole* and *Trakle*; in Moldavia the word for "vampire" is *drakul*; and in Hungary Vlad became known by a name that would endure for centuries—simply *Dracula*.

Clad in black velvet attire with an ominous dragon emblem on his

Bela Lugosi as the famous Count in Universal Pictures,
"Dracula." Copyright 1931.

Bela Lugosi uses his famous hypnotic powers in "Dracula."
Copyright 1931 by Universal Pictures.

chest and back, "Dracula" began to fatally torture an average of twelve persons per week, gradually developing an obsession with blood. He would impale his captives on stakes, cut their hands off, and let their blood drop into large copper vats. Then he would drink the blood, either straight or brewed with herbs and oftentimes blended with alcohol. A year before his death Dracula enjoyed the perverse act of biting women's jugular veins with his teeth. He enjoyed that method of killing, probably most of all.

Soon even Turkish Sultan Mahomet realized that Voivode Dracula must be destroyed for everyone's safety. But Vlad was not about to return his royal title. He nailed the Turkish representative's head down to the drawbridge of Ciglesz Castle. The Turks retaliated by sending an army to defeat him. Dracula, riding out to meet his attackers, raved insanely that the consumption of human blood made him invulnerable.

Backed by his army, Dracula was killed by the Turks who had given him his power, in the Battle of Oradea (1477).

Three years after Dracula's death, residents in the vicinity claimed that he had returned from the grave. The Voivode was reportedly seen dressed in ebony and mounted on his black horse, trotting along the mountain roads of Transylvania. It was said that Vlad smacked his lips, showing gleaming teeth and exclaiming that he thirsted for blood.

In the March 1968 issue of *Fate* magazine Leo Heiman interviewed a descendant of Voivode Dracula—Count Alexander Cepesi, a Rumanian expatriate. Cepesi operates, of all things, a blood bank, collecting plasma for Red Crescent agencies and Turkish hospitals, and dealing with blood sold for transfusion to people who desire the exclusiveness of a private clinic. The Count has resided in Istanbul since 1947.

Count Cepesi admitted the atrocities performed by his infamous ancestor. However, he ascribed vampirism to medical and not supernatural causes. "I have devoted a lifetime of study to vampires and their, history," Cepesi told his interviewer. "I had access to old family chronicles, ancient manuscripts and hair-raising tales handed down from generation to generation. I grew up in the very castle where the original Count Dracula committed his heinous crimes."

Dracula's life was hideous, stained by cauldrons of innocent blood. Yet his handsome portrait has found a place of honor in the Hungarian National Museum.

Supernatural vampire or not, the man who came to be known as "Dracula" was indeed a human monster.

An early woodcut of Vlad "the Impaler"—the original Count Dracula.

COUNTESS ELIZABETH BATHORY

The grim castle in the Carpathian Mountains was drowned in tradition of werewolves and other supernatural creatures. Within the gothic structure a room reeked with terror, a room whose windows and doors had been replaced by brick. There was a slit in the main wall through which food and water could be passed to the prisoner of the room. That prisoner was the most infamous female vampire in all history— Countess Elizabeth Bathory of Hungary.

The Bathory family had been known for its generations of sadists, witches, and sexual perverts. Elizabeth was born about the year 1560 into a family that included a sex fiend brother, a devil worshipper uncle, and a lesbian aunt. The young Elizabeth learned much from her weird assortment of relatives.

As Elizabeth grew older she became a practitioner of witchcraft. She carried with her at all times a parchment upon which was inscribed the following incantation against the police and government officials that she feared;

"*Isten*, help me! *Isten*, help me! You little cloud, help me too! Give me health, protection, and long life to Elizabeth. You little cloud, when I am in danger, send ninety-nine cats! I order you to do so because you are supreme commander of the cats. Give orders to the cats. Tell the cats to gather from wherever they be, on mountains, water, rivers, seas. Order ninety-nine cats to come with speed and bite the heart of King Matthias. Order them to bite the heart of Moses Cziraky, and to bite the heart of my cousin the prime minister. Command them to claw and bite the heart of Red Megyeri. And keep Elizabeth safe from harm."

Although the incantation was never fulfilled, the priest who had accompanied the police when they raided the Bathory castle on New Year's Eve in 1610 was mauled by six angry cats followed by a group of mice as he began walking up the front staircase.

Countess Elizabeth was not only the best known female living vampire; she was also the most, beautiful. Her black hair, contrasting with her pale complexion, followed her high cheek bones and draped to the waist of her voluptuous figure. In her amber eyes was the suggested slant of the eyes of a cat.

According to family custom the enticing young Countess married an aristocrat after turning fifteen. He was the bearded Count Ferencz Nadasdy who succumbed to the whims of this liberated woman and changed *his* name to "Bathory."

"As I was born a Bathory, she said with conviction, "so shall I live as a Bathory, and when I die I shall die as one."

The marriage lasted only a few years with the Count rarely spending time at the castle. He favored war to domestic life and destroyed the wounded and civilians with the same gusto he slew valiant warriors. Count Nadasdy spent more time away from his wife than with her. During Nadasdy's fighting periods Elizabeth gained her reputation as a bloodthirsty fiend.

Punishing and whipping servant girls satisfied Elizabeth's growing craving for blood—at first. But as she reached the age of twenty-six her lusts increased to more grisly proportions.

While Count Nadasdy was earning his future nickname "the Black Hero of Hungary," Elizabeth delved deeper and deeper into the mysteries of Black Magic, coached by a sorcerer named Thorke. She made no secret of her excursions into the darker realms of the occult. In a letter to her husband Elizabeth revealed:

"Thorko has taught me a lovely new one. Catch a black hen and beat it to death with a white cane. Keep the blood and smear a little of it on your enemy. If you get no chance to smear it on his body, obtain one of his garments and smear it."

About that time a stranger visited Elizabeth's castle when Count Nadasdy was busy on one of his battles. The stranger looked quite odd with his chalky skin, hard dark eyes, rather sharp teeth, and his black clothing. Immediately Elizabeth and the stranger became constant companions, while the neighboring peasants stayed indoors at night and bolted their locks. The stranger bore all the physical attributes of a supernatural vampire. Perhaps he was even Dracula back from the grave.

After a while the two eloped.

When the Countess returned to her husband, she was not with the mysterious stranger. Peasants claimed there were traces of fresh blood on her mouth as she spoke.

Count Nadasdy was still more concerned with real battles than one with his wife. He forgave her unfaithfulness as though it made no difference to him. Still they had no children. The Count mocked her saying that if she were indeed a powerful witch as she claimed, she could use her incantations to help produce offspring. His words could not go by unheeded. Elizabeth departed for the blackest section of the forest. There she stripped off her clothes, exposing her perfect body to the night, and performed a magical ceremony. Within the next four years Elizabeth bore the Count three boys and a girl.

Elizabeth's desires to see and feel warm blood increased almost beyond endurance. Her depraved mind, aided by the suggestions of an ugly hag named Ilona Joo, invented new methods by which to attain satisfaction. She began to experiment with new tortures. The spilling of human blood was developing into a science. Molten wax, knives, branding irons all broke the flesh of servant girls. Warned by both her husband and her mother-in-law to stop before the authorities had her executed, Elizabeth ignored them. Furthermore she recruited a whole team of tormentors—Johannes Uvjary the chief torturer, Thorko, and two notorious witches Dorottya Szentes and Darvula.

Count Nadasdy soon died, the suspected causes being witchcraft or poison. Elizabeth lost no time in ousting her mother-in-law from the castle.

The atrocities committed by the Countess were only beginning. She had turned forty years of age. Still a ravishing beauty Elizabeth became obsessed that she would soon become a wrinkled old woman. One day an accident occurred that instilled the most terrible idea of all in Elizabeth's warped mind. A maid was combing the Countess' long hair when she accidentally pulled it. Instinctively she slapped the girl so hard that blood spurted onto Elizabeth's hand. A wild look came upon her face. Elizabeth rubbed the blood between her fingers, smeared it into her pores. Her skin seemed to take on the servant's youth. Elizabeth had the answer to maintain her own youth; she must bathe in the blood of young virgins.

While the terrified maid stood in one corner of the chamber, Elizabeth summoned Johannes Uvjary and Thorko. Obeying the orders of their mistress they stripped the maid naked, cut her, and drained her blood into a vat. When the container was filled with red gore Elizabeth undressed and bathed ecstatically in the blood. When she emerged from the vat she could feel new-found youth and beauty course through her crimson stained body.

Now Countess Bathory needed a constant supply of young maidens. Her henchmen would prowl through the surrounding area to lure girls to the castle on the pretext of securing them jobs. When none of the girls ever returned no one would even approach the castle. Kidnaping was now the only resort to getting victims. Before Elizabeth was captured she had milked dry of blood from forty to three hundred young women.

For reasons unknown the authorities did not raid the castle to stop her evil practices.

Then one of Elizabeth's prisoners, barely alive, managed to escape with a too vivid account of what happened at the Bathory castle.

The girls were well fed and treated exquisitely—until it was their turn to satisfy the wants of the lesbian vampire. Their veins were pierced so their blood would flow. If they fainted pieces of flaming paper inserted between their toes awakened them so they would experience the total horror.

The atrocities of Countess Bathory and her crew of maniacs went on for ten years. But when a victim happened to be the daughter of a country priest's parishioner the clergyman demanded that King Matthias raid the castle. The King, infuriated beyond control, summoned the prime minister, a relative of Elizabeth. "Your cousin," said King Matthias, "is guilty not only of being a murderous fiend but of treason."

On that New Year's Eve when Countess Bathory and her accomplices were engaging in a frenzied orgy, the castle was invaded by her cousin and governor of the province Count Gyorgy Thurzo and a band of soldiers.

Elizabeth was confined to her house while her partners were all taken to jail.

The captured girls that still lived were freed.

The trial of Countess Bathory and her cohorts was indeed fascinating. Elizabeth was never present in the courtroom. She remained locked in her castle while the trial proceeded.

Despite the evidence affirming the practices of vampirism and witchcraft, the trial was held entirely on a criminal basis. Countess Bathory was accused of only physical crimes, without the inclusion of witchcraft, Black Magic, superstition, and hence free from hysteria, the enforced techniques of the Inquisition, or the supposed intervention of the devil.

The servants readily confessed all, as there was no way to lie considering the evidence against them.

Johannes Ujvary's testimony revealed much: As far as he knew thirty-seven unmarried girls were killed, six of which he personally acquired by telling them that servant jobs were available at the castle. After being tightly bound they were tied with tourniquets. Then their veins were slashed with scissors. Some of the girls were tortured by two old women Dorottya and Ilona, who were rewarded with gifts if they performed their bloody work well. Otherwise Countess Elizabeth tortured her victims unaided. The torments usually involved whippings and cutting with knives. Occasionally the victims were also frozen in icy water.

Ilona also testified: About forty girls had been tortured and killed. Heated coins and keys were sometimes placed in their hands. One girl's body was covered with honey. Sometimes when the girls were cut their blood would splash against the walls of the torture chamber.

Everyone involved—save for Elizabeth, Ilona Joo, and Dorottya Szentes—were beheaded and cremated. These latter two accomplices had their fingers yanked off individually, then were burned alive. Countess Bathory was found insane. Her sentence was thusly lightened to life imprisonment within her walled-up room. Within four years her worst dread became actualized. The once beautiful living vampire of Hungary had withered into an old hag. All of her blood bathing was to no avail.

In 1614 one of the guards stationed outside the great wall of brick peered through the slit provided for passing her food. He wanted to look at the infamous fiend whose beauty was once unchallenged but who was now an old woman.

The woman was lying on the floor, face down, unmoving. Countess Elizabeth Bathory was dead.

VAMPIRES OF SILESIA

Henry More, the famed Platonist of Cambridge, related the following histories of vampirism in Book III, chapter viii of his work *An Antidote Against Atheism: or, An Appeal to the Natural Faculties of the Mind of Man, whether there not be a God*, 1653. The first of his cases is as follows:

"A certain shoemaker in one of the chief towns of *Silesia*, in the year 1591, *Setemb.* 20, on a Friday betimes in the morning, in the further part of his house where there was adjoining a little Garden, cut his own Throat with his Shoemaker's knife. The family, to cover the foulness of the fact, and that no disgrace might come upon his Widow, gave out, that he died of an Apoplexy, declined all visits of friends and neighbours, in the meantime got him washed, and laid Linens so handsomely about him, that even they that saw him afterwards, as the Parson, and some others, had not the least Suspicion but that he did die of that disease; so he had honest Burial, with a funeral Sermon, and other circumstances becoming one of his rank and reputation. Six weeks had not past, but so strong a rumour broke out, that he died not of any disease, but had laid violent hands upon himself, that the Magistracy of the place could not but bring all those that had seen the corpse, to a strict examination. They shuffled off the matter as well as they could at first, with many fair Apologies, in behalf of the deceased, to remove all suspicion of so heinous an act: but it being pressed more home to their Conscience, at last they confessed, he dies a violent death, but desired their favour and clemency to his widow and children, who were in no fault; adding also, that it was uncertain but that he might be slain by some external mishap, or, if by himself, in some irresistible fit of phrency or madness.

"Hereupon the Council deliberate what is to be done. Which the Widow hearing, and fearing they might be determining something that would be harsh, to the discredit of her Husband, and herself, being also animated there to by some busie bodies, makes a great complaint against those that raised these reports of her Husband, and resolved to follow the Law upon them, earnestly contending that there was no reason, upon mere rumours and idle defamations of malevolent people, that her Husband's body should be digged up, or dealt with as if he had been either *Magician*, or *Self-murther*. Which boldness and pertinacity of the woman, though after the confession of the fact, did in some measure work upon the Council, and put them to a stand.

"But while these things were in agitation, to the astonishment of the Inhabitants of the place, there appears a *Spectrum* in the exact shape and habit of the deceased, and that not only in the night, but at midday. Those that were asleep it terrified with horrible visions; those that were waking it would strike, pull, or press, lying heavy upon them like an *Ephialtes*: so that there were perpetual complaints every morning of their last night's rest through the whole Town. But the more freaks this *Spectrum* play'd, the more diligent were the friends of the deceased to suppress the rumours of them or at least to hinder the effects of those rumours; and therefore made their addresses to the President, complaining how unjust a thing it was, that so much credit should be given to idle reports and blind suspicions, and therefore beseech'd him that he would hinder the Council from digging up the corpse of the deceased, and from all ignominious usage of him: adding also that they intended to appeal to the Emperor's Court, that their Wisdoms might rather decide the Controversy, than that the cause should be determined from the light conjectures of malicious men.

"But while by this means the business was still protracted, there were much stirs and tumults over the Town, that they are hardly to be described. For no sooner did the Sun hide its head, but this *Spectrum* would be sure to appear, so that every body was fain to look about him, and stand upon his guard, which was a sore trouble to those whom the Labours of the Day made more sensible of the want on rest in the night. For this terrible *Apparition* would sometimes stand by their bedsides, sometimes cast itself upon the midst of their beds, would lie close to them, would miserably suffocate them, and would so strike them and pinch them, that not only blue marks, but plain impressions of his fingers would be upon sundry parts of their bodies in the morning. Nay, such violence and impetuousness of this Ghost, that when men forsook their beds, and kept their dining-rooms, with Candles lighted, and many of them in company together, the better to secure themselves from fear and disturbance; yet he would then appear to them and have a bout with some of them, notwithstanding all this provision against it. In brief, he was so troublesome, that the people were ready to forsake their houses, and seek other dwellings, and the Magistrates so awakened at the perpetual complaints of them, that at last they resolved, the President agreeing thereto, to dig up the body.

"He had lain in the ground near eight months, *viz.* from *Sept.* 22, 1591, to *April* 18, 1592. When he was digged up, which was in the presence of the Magistracy of the Town, his body was found entire, not at all putrid, no ill smell about him saving the mustiness of the Gravecloaths , his joints limber and flexible, as in those that are alive, his skin only flaccid, but a more fresh grown in the room of it, the wound of his throat gaping, but no gear of corruption in it; there was also observed a Magical mark in the great toe of his right foot, *viz.* as Excrescency in the form of a Rose.

"His body was kept out of earth from *April* 18, to the 24th, at what time many both of the same town and others came daily to view him. These unquiet stirs did not cease for all of this, which they after attempted to appease, by burying the corpse under the Gallows, but in vain; for they were as much as ever, if not more, he now not sparing his own Family: insomuch that his Widow at last went her self to the Magistrate, and told them, that she should be no longer against it, if they thought fit to fall upon some course of more strict proceedings touching her husband.

"Wherefore the seventh of *May* he was again digged up, and it was observable, that he was grown more sensibly fleshy since his last interment. To be short, they cut off the Head, Arms, and Legs of the Corpse, and opening his Back, took out his heart, which was as fresh and intire as in a Calf new kill'd. These, together with his Body, they put on a pile of wood, and burnt them to Ashes, which they carefully sweeping together, and putting into a Sack (that non might get them for wicked uses) poured them into the River, after which the *Spectrum* was never seen more.

"As it also, happend in his Maid that dy'd after him, who appeared within eight days after her death, to her fellow servant, and lay so heavy upon her, that she brought upon her a great swelling of the eyes. She so grievously handled a Child in the cradle, that if the Nurse had not come to his help, he had been quite spoil'd; but she crossing her self, and calling upon the Name of *Jesus,* the Spectre vanished. The next night she appeared in the shape of a *Hen,* which, when one of the Maids of the house took to be so indeed, and followed her, the Hen grew into an immense bigness, and presently caught the Maid by the throat, and made it swell, so that she could neither eat nor drink of a good while after.

"She continued these stirs for a whole month, slapping some so smartly, that the stroke were heard of them that stood by, pulling the bed also from under others, and appearing sometime in one shape, sometimes in another, as of a Woman, of a Dog, of a Cat, and of a Goat. But at last her body was being digged up, and burnt, the Apparition was never seen more."

THE VAMPIRE OF PENTSCH: JOHANNES CUNTIUS

In his book against atheism Henry More also recounted the account of another Silesian vampire, Johannes Cuntius, whose hauntings had the attributes of a poltergeist:

"*Johannes Cuntius,* a Citizen of *Pentsch* in *Silesia,* near sixty years of age, and one of the *Aldermen* of the Town, very fair in his carriage, and unblameable, to men's thinking, in the whole course of his life, having been sent for to the *Mayor's* house (as being a very understanding man, and dexterous at the dispatch of businesses) to end some controversies concerning certain. Waggoners, and a Merchant of *Pannonia* having made an end of those affairs, is invited by the Mayor to Supper: he gets leave first to go home to order some businesses, leaving this sentence behind him, *It's good to be merry while we may, for mischiefs grow up fast enough daily.*

"This *Cuntius* kept five lusty Geldings in his Stable, one whereof he commanded to be brought out, and his shoe being loose, had him ty'd to the next post: his Master with a Servant busied themselves to take up his leg to look on his hoof, the Horse being mad and mettlesome, struck them both down; but *Cuntius* received the greatest share of the blow: one that stood next by help'd them both up again. *Cuntius* no sooner was up and came to him self, but cry'd out, *Wo is me, how do I burn, and am all on a fire!* which he often repeated. But the parts he complain'd of most, the Women being put out of the room, when they were searched, no appearance of any stroke or hurt was found upon them. To be short, he fell downright sick, and grievously afflicted in Mind, loudly complaining, that his Sins were such, that they were utterly unpardonable, and that the least part of them were bigger than all the Sins of the World besides; but would have no Divine come to him, nor did particularly confess them to any. Several rumours indeed there were that once he had sold one of his Sons, but when, and to whom, it was uncertain; and that he had made a Contract with the Devil, and the like. But it was observed, and known for certain, that he had grown beyond all expectation rich, and that four days before his mischance, he being witness to a Child, said that that was the last he should be ever witness to.

"The night he dy'd, his eldest Son watched with him. He gave up the Ghost about the third hour of the night, at what time a black Cat, opening the casement with her nails (for it was shut) ran to his bed, and did so violently scratch his face and the bolster, as if she endeavored by force to remove him out of the place where he lay. But the Cat afterwards suddenly was gone, and she was no sooner gone, but he breathed his last. A fair Tale was made to the Pastor of the Parish, and the Magistracy of the Town allowing it, he was buried on the right side of the Altar, his Friends paying well for it. No sooner *Cuntius* was dead, but a great Tempest arose, which raged most at his very Funeral, there being such impetuous Storms of Wind with Snow, that it made men's bodies quake, and their teeth chatter in their heads. But so soon as he was interred, of a sudden all was calm.

"He had not been dead a day or two, but several rumours were spread in the town of a *Spiritus incubus*, or *Ephialtes*, in the shape of *Cuntius*, that would have forced a Woman. This happen'd before he was buried. After his burial, the same Spectre awaken'd one that was sleeping in his dining room, saying, *I can scarce withhold my self from beating thee to death.* The voice was the voice of *Cuntius*. The watchmen of the

Town also affirmed, that they heard every night great stirs in Cuntius his House, the fallings and throwings of things about, and that they did see the gates stand wide open betimes in the mornings, though they were never so diligently shot o'er night; that his Horses were very unquiet in the Stable, as if they kick'd, and bit one another; besides unusual barkings and howlings of the Dogs all over the Town. But these were but preludious suspicions to further evidence, which I will run over as briefly as I may.

"A Maid-servant of one of the Citizens of *Pentsch* (while these Tragedies and Stirs were so frequent in the Town) heard, together with some others lying in their beds, the noise and tramplings of one riding about the House, who at last ran against the Walls with that violence, that the whole House shaked again, as if it would fall, and the windows were all fill'd with flashings of light. The Master of the house being informed of it, went out of doors in the morning to see what the matter was; and he beheld in the Snow the impressions of strange feet, such as were like neither Horses, nor Cows, nor Hogs, nor any Creature that he knew.

"Another time, about eleven o'clock in the night, *Cuntius* appears to be one of his Friends that was a witness to a Child of his, speaks unto him, and bids him to be of good courage, for he came only to communicate unto him a matter of great importance. *I have left behind me, said he, my youngest Son James, to whom you are Godfather. Now there is my eldest Son Steven's, a Citizen of Jegerdorf, a certain Chest, wherein I have put four hundred and fifteen Florens: This I tell you, that your God-son may not be defrauded of any of them, and it is your duty to look after it; which if you neglect, wo be to you.* Having said this, the *Spectre* departed, and went up into the upper rooms of the House, where he walked so stoutly that all rattled again, and the roof swagged with his heavy stampings. This *Cuntius* his Friend told to the Parson of the Parish a day or two after a certain truth.

"But there were also several other notorious passages of this *Cuntius*. As is often speaking to the Maid that lay with her Mistress, his Widow, to give him place, for it was his right; and if she would not give it to him, he would writh her neck behind her.

"His galloping up and down like a wanton horse in the Court of his House. He being divers times seen to ride, not only in the streets, but along the vallies of the fields, and on the Mountains, with so strong a trot, that he made the very ground flash with fire under him.

"His bruising of the body of a Child of a certain Smiths, and making his very bones so soft, that you might wrap the corpse on heaps like a glove.

"His miserable tugging all night with a *Jew* that had taken up his Inn in the Town, and tossing him up and down in the lodging where he lay.

"His dreadful accosting of a Waggoner, an old acquaintance of his, while he was busie in the stable, vomiting out fire against him to terrify him, and biting of him so cruelly by the foot, that he made him lame.

"What follows, as I above intimated, concerns the Realtor himself, who was the Parson of the Parish, whom his Fury so squeez'd and press'd when he was asleep, that wakening he found himself utterly spent, and his strength quite gone, but could not imagine the reason. But while he lay musing with himself what the matter might be, this *Spectre* returns again to him, and holding him all over so fast, that he could not wag a finger, rowled him in his bed backwards and forwards a good many times together. The same happen'd also to his Wife another time, whom *Cuntius*, coming thro' the casement in the shape of a little Dwarf, and running to her bed-side, so wrung and pulled as if he would have torn her throat out, had not her two Daughters come in to help her.

"He pressed the lips together of one of this *Theologer's* Sons so, that they could scarce get them asunder.

"His House was so generally disturbed with this unruly Ghost, that the Servants were fain to keep together anights in one room, lying upon straw, and watching the approaches of this troublesome Fiend. But a Maid of the House, being more courageous than the rest, would needs one night go to bed, and forsake her company. Where upon *Cuntius* finding her alone, presently assaults her, pulls away the bedding, and would have carried her away with him; but she hardly escaping fled to the rest of the family, where she espied him standing by the candle, and straightway after vanishing.

"Another time he came into her Master's Chamber, making a noise like a Hog that eats grain, smacking and grunting very sonorously. They could not chase him away, by speaking to him; but ever as they lighted a Candle, he would vanish.

"On another Time about Evening, when this *Theologer* was sitting with his Wife and Children about him, exercising himself in Musick, according to his usual manner, a most grievous stink arose suddenly, which by degrees spread itself to every corner of the room. Here upon he commends himself and his family to God by Prayer. The smell nevertheless encreased, and became above all measure, pestilently noisom, insomuch that he was forced to go up to his chamber. He and his Wife had not been in bed a quarter of an hour, but they find the same stink in the bed-chamber; of which, while they are complaining one to another, out steps the Spectre from the Wall, and creeping to his bed-side, breathes upon him an exceeding cold breath, of so intolerable stinking and malignant a scent, as is beyond all imagination and expression. Here upon the *Theologer*, good soul, grew very ill, and was fain to keep his bed, his face, belly, and guts swelling as if he had been poysoned; whence he was also troubled with a difficulty of breathing, and with a putrid inflammation of his eyes, so that he could not well use them of a long time after.

"But taking leave of the sick Divine, if we should go back, and recount what we have ommitted, it would exceed the number of what we have already recounted. As for example, The trembling and sweating of *Cuntius* his Gelding, from which he was not free night nor day: The burning blue of the Candles at the approaches of *Cuntius* his Ghost: His drinking up the milk in the milk-bowls, his flinging dung into them, or turning the milk into blood: His pulling up posts deep set in the ground, and so heavy, that two lusty Porters could not deal with them: his discoursing with several men he met concerning the affairs of the Waggoners: His strangling of old men: His holding fast the Cradles of Children, or taking them out of them: His frequent endeavoring to force women: His defiling the Water in the Font, and fouling the Cloth on the Altar on that side that did hang towards his grave with dirty bloody spots: His catching up Dogs in the streets, and knocking their brains against the ground: His sucking dry the Cows, and tying their tails like the tail of an Horse: His devouring of Poultry, and his flinging of Goats bound into the Racks: His tying of an Horse to an empty oat-tub in the Stable, to clatter up and down with it, and the hinder foot of another to his own head-stall: His looking out of the Window of a low Tower, and then suddenly changing himself into the form of a long staff: His chiding of a Matron for suffering her servant to wash dishes on a Thursday, at what time he laid his hand upon her, and she said, it felt more cold than ice: His pelting one of the Women that washed his corpse, so forcibly, that the prints of the Clods he flung, were to be seen upon the wall: His attempting to ravish another, who excusing herself and saying, *My Cuntius, thou seest how old, wrinkled, and deformed I am, and how unfit for those kind of sports*, he suddenly set up a loud laughter, and vanished.

"But we must insist upon these things; only we will add one passage more that is not a little remarkable. His gravestone was turned of one

side, shelving, and there were several holes in the earth, about the bigness of mouse-holes, that went down to his very Coffin, which, however
they were filled up with earth over night, yet they would be sure to be
laid open in the morning.

"It would be a tedious business to recite these things at large, and,
prosecute the Story in all its particular Circumstances. To conclude
therefore, their calamity as such, from the frequent occursions of this
restful fury, that there was none but either pitied them, or despis'd
them; none would lodge in their Town, Trading was decay'd, and the
Citizens impoverished by the continual stirs and tumults of this unquiet Ghost.

"And though the *Atheist* may perhaps laugh at them, as men un-
done by their own Melancholy and vain imaginations, or by the wag-
gery of some ill neighbors; yet if he seriously consider what has been
already related, there are many passages that are by no means to be
resolved into any such Principles; but what I shall now declare, will
make it altogether unlikely that any of them are.

"To be short, therefore, finding no rest, nor being able to excogitate
any better remedy, they dig up *Cuntius* his body with several others
buried both before and after him. But those both after and before were
so putrify'd and rotten, their Skulls broken, and the Sutures of them
gaping, that they were not to be known by their shapes at all, having
become in a manner but a rude mass of earth and dirt; but it was quite
otherwise in *Cuntius*: His Skin was tender and florid, his joynts not at
all stiff, but limber and moveable, and a staff being put into his hand,
he grasped it with His fingers very fast; his Eyes also of themselves
would be one time open, and another time shut; they opened a vein in
his Leg, and the blood sprang out as fresh as in the living; his Nose was
entire and full, not sharp, as in those that are ghastly sick, or quite
dead: and yet Cuntius his body had lien in the grave from *Feb.* 8 to *July*
20 which is almost half a year.

"It was easily discernible where the fault lay. However, nothing
done rashly, but judges were constituted, Sentence was pronounced upon
Cuntius his Carcase, which (being animated thereto from success in the
like case, some few years before in this very Province of *Silesia*, I suppose he means *Breslaw*, where the Shoemakers body was burnt) they
adjudged to the fire.

"Wherefore there were Masons provided to make a hole in the wall
near the Altar to get his body through, which being pulled at with a
rope, it was so exceeding heavy, that the rope brake, and they could

scarce stir him. But when they had pull'd him through, and gotten him on a Cart without, which *Cuntius* his Horse had struck him (which was a lusty-boiled jade) was to draw; yet it put him to it so, that he was ready to fall down ever and anon, and was quite out of breath with striving to draw so intolerable a load, who not withstanding could run away with two men in the same Cart presently after, their weight was so inconsiderable to his strength.

"His body, when it was brought to the fire, proved as unwilling to be burnt, as before to be drawn; so that the Exicutioner was fain with hooks to pull him out, and cut him into pieces to make him burn. Which, while he did, the blood was found so pure and spiritous, that it spurted into his face as he cut him; but at last not without the expence of two hundred and fifteen great billets, all was turned into ashes. Which they carefully sweeping up together, as in the foregoing Story, and casting them into the River, the Spectre never more appeared.

"I must confess, I am so low witted myself that I cannot so much as imagine, what the *Atheist* will excogitate for a subterfuge or hiding place, from so plain and evident Convictions."

VAMPIRE LOVER OF PARIS?

After visiting a group of friends a young Parisian returned home about four o'clock on 1 January 1613. As it had begun to rain he hastened to his house. But as he approached the familiar building he noticed an appealing sight. A woman, seemingly wealthy as evidenced by her embroidered silk gown, her pearls, her jeweled necklaces, rings, and pins, was seated upon the porch leading to his door. The woman apologized for trespassing but said she was merely attempting to avoid the rain. She only wished to intrude until her servant returned with her carriage.

The young main said that she was not intruding. Furthermore, if she wished, it would please him if she waited inside. The woman paused in deliberation, protesting that it would not be proper. But when the rain continued pouring down she at last agreed to go within.

As the time passed the servant failed to return. It was already meal time. Preparing a substantial dinner, the young man served it to his guest and the two ate well.

The storm did not subside and the servant seemed lost. Rather than send the woman into the storm at such a late hour the young man offered her shelter for the night in a separate room. Again she consented.

After the servants of the house left for the night, the host entered the woman's room, asking if she were comfortable. He took her hand, kissed her, and before long the two were sharing a night of love. Afterwards the Parisian returned to his own room.

The following morning the young host told a servant to see to the needs of the woman. The servant came back with word that the guest, tired from lack of sleep, did not wish to get out of bed so early. After a refreshing walk outside the young man himself ventured into her room. He whispered romantic sayings through the curtain, then pulled it aside, but received no answer. Concerned, he grasped her hand finding it as cold as stone. The woman was dead.

The Parisian immediately summoned some doctors, along with the magistrate. To their horror they identified the corpse as a woman who had been hanged some time before. The men concluded that the creature was a vampire, caused either by possession of a devil or spectre or by a return of the spirit of the woman herself, who wanted to satisfy her desires even after death. As they were speaking a dense cloud of smoke, arose from the bed, settled for several moments, then vanished along with the body.

The case was recorded by Dudley Wright in his *Vampires and Vampirism.*

VAMPIRES OF GERMANY

Cases of vampirism have often been recorded in certain areas of Germany, primarily in West Prussia.

In 1617 a citizen of the town of Egwanschiftz was the victim of a vampire, being both tormented and bitten by the creature. When the victim finally died due to repeated visitations, both his corpse and that of the vampire were cremated on the outskirts of the town.

A rich landowner in 1820, owning much property in the Danzig area, was also frequented by the presence of a vampire. Only the prayers and sacrifices of the Cistercian monks, who had been ousted from their house on 28 April 1810 by proclamation of the Prussian government, brought a halt to the creature's visitations.

When a terrible epidemic of cholera broke out in Danzig in 1855, death was attributed to the attacks of vampires. Reports have it that many people died not from actual disease but from fright.

A Friendly Vrykolakas

A woman living on the island of Santorini was occasionally visited by her husband, who had long since died and become a vampire—one of the *vrykolakes*.

The man, named Alexander, had lived as a cobbler in the tiny village of Prygos. After his death Alexander continued to visit his wife, resembling a living man and performing a number of chores. He brought home buckets of water from the reservoir, mended the shoes of his own children, and went out into the woods to chop wood.

The villagers, terrified that a *vrykolakas* was prowling about the vicinity, decided that Alexander must be destroyed. They exhumed his corpse. Finding it in the vampire state, they burned it, sending the power of the *vrykolakas* into a spreading cloud of dark smoke.

The account was given by a Jesuit priest, Father Francois Richard, in his *Relation de l'isle de Sant-erinin*, 1657.

It should be noted that Santorini is known for vampiric hauntings. The island is the farthest south of the Cyclades, sixty miles north of Crete.

In the seventh edition of *Murray's Handbook for Travellers in Greece*, 1900, the author says of Santorini:

"The antiseptic nature of the soil, and the frequent discovery of undecayed bodies, have given rise to many wild superstitions among the peasantry of the island. It is supposed to be the favourite abode of the *Vrykolakas* a species of Ghoul or Vampire, which, according to a belief once popular in Greece, has the power of resuscitating the dead from their graves and sending them forth to banquet on the living."

THE VAMPIRE
OF CROGLIN GRANGE

One of the most well-known accounts of vampirism was given by Captain Fisher to August Hare, who included the report in his *Story of Life*. Originally the history was dated 1875 but is included in this chronological position for reasons explained later.

"Fisher may sound a very plebian name, but this family is of a very ancient lineage, and for many hundreds of years they have possessed a very curious old place in Cumberland, which bears the weird name of Croglin Grange. The great characteristic of the house is that never at any period of its very long existence has it been more than one story high, but it has a terrace from which large grounds sweep away towards the church in the hollow, and a fine distant view.

"When, in lapse of years, the Fishers outgrew Croglin Grange in family and fortune, they were wise enough not to destroy the long-standing characteristic of the place by adding another story to the house, but they went away to the south, to reside at Thomcombe near Guildford, and they let Croglin Grange.

"They were extremely fortunate in their tenants, two brothers and a sister. They heard their praises from all quarters. To their poorer neighbours they were all that is most kind and beneficent, and their neighbours of a higher class spoke of them as a most welcome addition to the little society of the neighbourhood. On their part, the tenants were greatly delighted with their new residence. The arrangement of the house, which would have been a trial to many, was not so to them. In every respect Croglin Grange was exactly suited to them.

"The winter was spent most happily by the new inmates of Croglin Grange, who shared in all the little social pleasures of the district, and made themselves very popular. In the following summer there was one day which was dreadfully, annihilatingly hot. The brothers lay under the trees with their books, for it was too hot for any active occupation. The sister sat in the veranda and worked, or tried to work, for the intense sultriness of that summer day, work was next to impossible. They dined early, and after dinner that still sat out on the veranda, enjoying the cool air which came with evening, and they watched the sun set, and the moon rise over the belt of trees which separated the grounds from the churchyard, seeing it mount the heavens till the whole

Max Schreck is reminiscent of the vampire of Croglin Grange in the 1922 film "Nosferatu."

lawn was bathed in silver light, across which the long shadows from the shrubbery fell as if embossed, so vivid and distinct they were.

"When they separated for the night, all retiring to their rooms on the ground floor (for, as I said, there was no upstairs in that house), the sister felt that the heat was still so great that she could not sleep, and having fastened her window, she did not close the shutters—in that very quiet place it was not necessary—and, propped against the pillows, she still watched the wonderful, the marvellous beauty of that summer night. Gradually she became aware of two lights, two lights which flickered in and out in the belt of trees which separated the lawn from the church-yard, and, as her gaze became fixed upon them, she saw them emerge, fixed in a dark substance, a definite ghastly *something*, which seemed every moment to become nearer, increasing in size and substance as it approached. Every now and then it was lost for a moment in the long shadows which stretched across the lawn from the trees, and then it emerged larger than ever, and still coming on. She longed to get away, but the door was close to the window, and the door was locked on the inside, and while she was unlocking it she must be for an instant nearer to it. She longed to scream, but her voice seemed paralysed, her tongue glued to the roof of her mouth.

"Suddenly—she could never explain why afterwards—the terrible object seemed to turn to one side, seemed to be going round the house, not to be coming to her at all, and immediately she jumped out of bed and rushed to the door, but as she was unlocking it she heard scratch, scratch, scratch upon the window, and saw a hideous brown face with flaming eyes glaring in at her. She rushed back to the bed, but the creature continued to scratch, scratch, scratch upon the window. She felt a sort of mental comfort in the knowledge that the window was securely fastened on the inside. Suddenly the scratching sound ceased, and a kind of pecking sound took its place. Then, in her agony, she became aware that the creature was unpicking the lead! The noise continued, and a diamond pane of glass fell into the room. Then a long bony finger of the creature came in and turned the handle of the window, and the window opened, and the creature came in; and it came across the room, and her terror was so great that she could not scream, and it came up to the bed, and it twisted its long bony finger into her hair, and it dragged her head over the side of the bed, and—it bit her violently in the throat.

"As it bit her, her voice was released, and she screamed with all her might and main. Her brothers rushed out of their rooms, but the door was locked on the inside. A moment was lost while they got a poker and broke it open. Then the creature had already escaped through the window, and the sister, bleeding violently from a wound in the throat, was lying unconscious over the side of the bed. One brother pursued the creature, which fled before him through the moonlight with gigantic strides, and eventually seemed to disappear over the wall into the churchyard. Then he rejoined his brother by the sister's bedside. She was dredfully hurt, and her wound was a very definite one, but she was of strong disposition, not even given to romance or superstition, and when she came to herself she said, 'What has happened is most extraordinary and I am very much hurt. It seems inexplicable, but of course there is an explanation, and we must wait for it. It will turn out that a lunatic has escaped from some asylum and found his way here.' The wound healed, and she appeared to get well, but the doctor who was sent for to her would not believe that she could bear so terrible a shock so easily, and insisted that she must have a change, mental and physical; so her brothers took her to Switzerland.

"Being a sensible girl, when she went abroad she threw herself at once into the interests of the country she was in. She dried plants, she made sketches, she went up mountains, and, as autumn came on, she was the person who urged that they should return to Croglin Grange. 'We have taken it,' she said, 'for seven years, and we have only been there one; and we shall always find it difficult to let a house which is only one story high, so we had better return there; lunatics do not escape every day.' As she urged it, her brothers wished nothing better, and the family returned to Cumberland. From there being no upstairs in the house it was impossible to make any great change in their arrangements. The sister occupied the same room, but it was unnecessary to say she always closed the shutters, which, however, as in many old houses, always left one top pane of the window uncovered. The brothers moved, and occupied a room together, exactly opposite that of their sister, and they always kept loaded pistols in their room.

"The winter passed most peacefully and happily. In the following March, the sister was suddenly awakened by a sound she remembered only too well—scratch, scratch, scratch upon the window, and looking up, she saw, climbed up to the topmost pane of the window, the same hideous brown shriveled face, with glaring eyes, looking in at her. This time she screamed as loud as she could. Her brothers rushed out of their room with pistols, and out of the front door. The creature was already scudding away across the lawn. One of the brothers fired and hit it in the leg, but still with the other leg it continued to make sway, scrambled over the wall into the churchyard, and seemed to disappear into a vault which belonged to a family long extinct.

"The next day the brothers summoned all the tennants of Croglin Grange, and in their presence the vault was opened. A horrible scene revealed itself. The vault was full of coffins; they had been broken open, and their contents, horribly mangled and distorted, were scattered over the floor. One coffin alone remained intact. Of that the lid had been lifted, but still lay loose upon the coffin. They raised it, and there, brown, withered, shriveled, mummified, but quite entire, was the same hideous figure which had looked in at the windows of Croglin Grange, with the marks of a recent pistol-shot in the leg: and they did the only thing that can lay a vampire—they burnt it."

The account of the Croglin Grange vampire has been severely criticized for authenticity. Three main objections were listed by Charles G. Harper in his book *Haunted Houses* published in 1924. Harper stated that 1) there is no place called Croglin Grange: 2) there are Croglin Low all and Croglin High Hall, but both are two story buildings, contradicting the report; and 3) the church is at least a mile away—rebuilt in1878, it "contains no tomb which by any stretch of imagination would be identified with that described by Mr. Hare."

More recently, in the June, 1967 issue of *Fate* magazine, the account was criticized by D. Scott Rogo. His dissatisfaction with the narrative primarily involved the sixth paragraph's resemblance to the first chapter of Thomas Preskett Prest's 1847 romance *Varney the Vampire*. Rogo deduced that the Croglin Grange account was a plagiarism of *Varney*. The similarity in sentences in the two are remarkable, as evidenced by the following excerpt from *Varney*.

"It is its fingernails upon the glass that produces sound so like the hail ... a small pane of glass is broken and the form introduces a long gaunt hand. The fastening is removed and one half of the window, which opens like folding doors, is swung wide open upon its hinges— and yet now she could not scream ... The terrible object seemed to turn to one side ... It approached the bed ... The figure seized the long tresses of hair and twining them around his bony hands, he held her to the bed ... He drags her head to the bed's edge—he seized her neck in his fanglike teeth ..."

Rogo contended that the only logical explanation is that Captain Fisher concocted the story in order to produce another tourist attraction with the appeal of many British haunted houses. But Rogo subsequently had new feelings that the Croglin Grange account may be authentic. In an issue of *Tomorrow* magazine F. Clive-Ross investigated the case to prove once and for all if it were fact or fraud.

F. Clive-Ross personally journeyed to the vicinity where the occurrence was to have taken place. First visiting the church, he noticed a printed sheet on the porch which gave its history in brief. At the bottom of the sheet was the information "Croglin Low Hall is the ancient Manor House of Little Croglin. It belonged to the Dacre family until 1589. There was a second church in Croglin here, probably serving as a private chapel to the house. Nothing of this church now exists. The house is now a farm." The implications were pertinent. If a church once existed near Croglin Low Hall, the current church of a mile away would not even enter into the case.

Further investigation on a personal level brought him to the very room in which the vampire is said to have bitten the girl. The windows were more recent Eighteenth Century, altered considerably from the original leaded plane design, indicating that the house was *raised one story* in 1720 when the vampire window was blocked up. This blocking pre-dates Varney the Vampire well over a century.

An interview with a Mrs. Parkins gave him still more information asserting the authenticity of the account. According to Mrs. Parkins the ruined foundation of the original church could be seen as late as 1933. The vampire story, she said, actually dated between 1680 and 1690. Local tradition reveals graves, including a Fisher vault, in the churchyard. Also, one of the men who was present at the cremation had a previous encounter with the monster, wherein his three-year-old daughter was bitten by the creature. Mrs. Parkins had known a member of the Fisher family born in the 1860's, who had heard the vampire story from his grandparents, and said that the blocked-up vampire window had been such as far back as he could recall. In conclusion she stated that, according to the deeds of Croglin Low Hall, until the year 1720 the name commonly used was Croglin Grange!

F. Clive-Ross seems to have contradicted and disproved the three objections of Charles G. Harper in favor of the vampire, along with D. Scott Rogo's theory that the account plagiarized *Varney the Vampire*.

GRANDO,
VAMPIRE OF CARNIOLA

In Erasmus Franciscus' commentary on Baron Valvasor's 1689 work *Die Ehre des Herzogthums Krain*, Ljubljana, there is an account of a vampire in Carniola.

A peasant named Grando lived in the district of Kranj as a hard-working, well liked man. His death, however, was followed by the infection of a vampire which satisfied its thirst on the blood of the villagers. Everyone in Carniola realized, because of the timing, that the vampire had to be Grando.

With the permission of the Church, Grando's body was exhumed and discovered in the horribly familiar vampire form. The complexion was ruddy like that of a man alive. The face quivered, then curled into a cruel grin, taking in a breath of new air. His eyes popped open. Terrified by the uncanny phenomenon the people at the grave began to pray, as the priest approached the body, extending a Crucifix. Armed with this holy weapon the priest pronounced these words over the monster:

"Raise thine eyes and look upon Jesus Christ who hath redeemed us from the pains of hell by His most Holy Passion and His precious Death upon the Rood."

Grando's features altered to an expression of utter sorrow. Considering the actions of the priest the vampire wept.

Solemnly the priest prayed for the creature's soul, that it might be saved. An attempt was made to drive a stake of hawthorne through his body but the shaft was not effective. At last Grando was beheaded, his body giving a final twitch as though alive.

A similar case was recorded in Dudley Wright's *Vampires and Vampirism*.

"At one time the spectre of a village herdsman near Kodom, in Bavaria, began to appear to several inhabitants of the place, and either in consequence of their fright or from some other cause, every person who had seen the apparition died during the week afterwards. Driven to despair, the peasants disinterred the corpse and pinned it to the ground with a long stake. The same night he appeared again, plunging people into convulsions of fright, and suffocated several of them. Then the village authorities handed the body over to the executioner, who caused it to be carried into a field adjoining the cemetery, where it was burned. The corpse howled like a madman, kicking and tearing as if it had been alive. When it was through again with sharp-pointed stakes, before the burning, it uttered piercing cries and vomited masses of crimson blood. The apparition of the spectre ceased only after the corpse had been reduced to ashes."

CREMATION
OF A VROUCOLACAS

The methods by which the vampire meets destruction are numerous, for even the most universal techniques differ in regards detail with the particular culture. Cremation seems to have worldwide effectiveness against undead monsters.

French botanist Joseph Pitton de Toumefort was on his way to the Orient, a journey lasting from 1700 to 1702. In his classic *Relations d'um Voyage du Levant* in two volumes, Paris, 1717, the eminent botanist reported:

"We witnessed an entirely different and very tragic scene in this same island, Myconos, in connexion with one of those dead men who, as they confidently believe, return after they have been buried. The man, whose story we are going to relate, was a peasant of Myconos, in disposition naturally curlish and very quarrelsome, and this is a detail which is worth noting, for it often occurs in similar instances. This man, then, was murdered in some lonely country place, and nobody knew how, or by whom. Two days after he had been buried in a small chapel or oratory in the town it began to be noised abroad that he had been set at nights walking about with great hasty strides, that he went into houses, and tumbled about all the furniture, that he extinguished candles and lamps, that he suddenly fast gripped hold of people behind and wrought a thousand other mischiefs and very knaveries. At first people sometimes laughed at the tale, but when the graver and more respectable citizens began to complain of these assaults the affair became truly serious. The Greek priests candidly acknowledged the fact of these disturbances, and perhaps, they had their own reasons for so doing. A number of masses were duly said, but in spite of it all, hob the peasant continued to drive his old trade and scarcely showed himself at all inclined to mend his ways for all that they could do. The leading citizens of the district, a number of priests and monks met together to discuss the business several times, and in accordance with some ancient ritual of which I do not know the purport, they decided that they must wait for a clear nine days after the burial.

"On the next day, the tenth, a solemn mass was sung in the chapel where the body lay in order to appeal the demon, who, as they believed, had taken possession of it. The body was exhumed after the mass, and presently everything was ready to tear out the heart, according to custom. The town flesher, an old and clumsy-fisted fellow, began by ripping open the belly instead of the breast: he groped a good while among the entrails without finding what he sought, and then at last somebody informed him that he must dissever the diaphragm. So the heart was finally extracted amid the wonder and applause of all who were present. But the carrion now stank so foully that they were obliged to burn a large quantity of frankincense, when the hot fume commingled with the bad gases that were escaping from the putrid corpse but served to augment and extend the fetor which seemed to mount to the brains of those who were intent upon the loathy spectacle. Their heated imaginations reeled, and the rank horror of the thing inflamed their minds with wild fantasies. Some even commenced to cry aloud that a thick cloud of smoke was being spewed out by the dead body, and in sober sooth amid the frenzy we did not dare to assert that this was merely the thick fume pouring from the thuribles. Throughout the whole chapel, then, and in the square which lies before it, one heard nothing but *Vroucolacas*, for this is the name that is given to these persons who return in this evil wise. The bawling and noise spread throughout all the neighbouring streets and this name was shouted so loudly that it seemed to cleave the very vault of the chapel itself. Many of the bystanders asserted that the blood of this poor wretch was a rich vermil red in hue; whilst the flesher swore that the body was still quite warm as in life. Thereupon all mightily blamed the dead man for not being really dead, or rather for allowing his body to be re-animated by the devil, for this is the true idea they have of a *Vroucolacas*. As I have said, this name re-echoed on every side in a most extraordinary manner. Large numbers of people went up and down through the crowd asserting that they could clearly see that the body was still supple with pliant unstiffened limbs when they bore it from the fields to the church to bury it, and that he was obviously a most malignant *Vroucolacas*. One could hear nothing but that word being repeated over and over again.

"I am very certain that if we had not ourselves been actually present these folk would have maintained that there was no stench of corruption, to such an extent were the poor people terrified and amazed and obsessed with the idea that dead men are able to return. As for ourselves, we had carefully taken up a position quite near the body in order that we might exactly observe what took place, and we were retching and well nigh overcome by the stench of the rotting corpse. When we were asked what we thought about this dead man, we replied that we certainly believed he was indeed dead, but as we wished to soothe or at least not to inflame their diseased imaginations we tried to convince them that there was nothing at all extraordinary in what had taken place, that it was hardly surprising the flesher should have felt a degree of warmth, as he fumbled with his hands amid the decomposing viscera; that it was quite usual for mephitic gases to escape from a dead man just as they issue from an old midden when the heap is stirred or moved; as for this bright red blood which still stained the flesher's hands and arms 'twas but foul-smelling clots of filth and gore!

"But in spite of all our arguments and all our reasoning a little later they burned the dead man's heart on the seashore, and yet in spite of this cremation he was even more aggressive, and caused more dire vexation and confusion than before. It was commonly reported that every night he beat folk sorely; he broke down doors and even the roofs of houses; he clattered at and burst in windows; he tore jerkins and dresses to rags; he emptied all the jugs and bottles. 'Twas the most thirsty devil! I believe that he did not spare anyone except the consul in whose house we lodged. Howbeit I have never seen anything more pitiful and sad than the state of this island. All the people were scared out of their wits, and the wisest and best among them were just as terrorized as the rest. It was an epidemic disorder of the brain, as dangerous as a mania or as sheer lunacy. Whole families left their houses and from the furthest suburbs of the town brought little tentbeds and pallets into the public square, in order to pass the night in the open. Each moment somebody was complaining of some fresh vexation or assault; when night fell nothing was to be heard but cries and groans; the better sort of people withdrew into the country.

"At such a crisis and in the midst of so great confusion and mortal alarm, we resolved to hold our peace, making no comment and proferring no opinion. It is certain that for any criticism not only should we have been considered shallow and ignorant fools, but more, we should have been regarded as godless atheists. It was entirely out of our power to counteract the effects of an old and common tradition. Those who shrewdly suspected that we had grave doubts with regard to the true explanation of what had occurred used to visit us with the obvious intentions of rebuking our unbelief, and they have made it their business to prove that there actually were Vroucolacas by the evidence of various authorities whom they quoted from *The Shield of Faith*, a work by Father Richard, a Jesuit missionary. 'He was a Latin, a Roman of Rome,' they insisted, 'and consequently you most surely ought to believe him.' We did not attempt to deny the logic of their argument, and so every morning they kept coming to us with their tale, an exact relation of some fresh assault which this night-bird had committed, some new plague or vexation; they even accused him of the most hideous and abominable crimes.

"Those inhabitants who had the public good sincerely at heart believed that a mistake had been made in one of the essential points of the ceremony, for in their opinion the Mass should not have been celebrated until they had extracted the heart from the corpse of this vile wretch; they were quite certain that if this precaution had been taken the devil must inevitably have been caught and that he could not have re-entered the dead body, instead of which, since the officiants had begun by celebrating the Mass first of all, the devil, according to their idea, had found ample opportunity to escape and then when the liturgy was over there was nothing to hinder him from returning at will.

"The sole result of these discussions was that they found themselves exactly in the same difficulty as they were at the beginning. Night and morning the village council met; they deliberated at great length. Solemn processions paraded the streets for three days and three nights; all the priests most rigidly fasted; they continually went from house to house each carrying his aspergillun in his hand, sprinkling holy water and washing the doors with it; they even poured a quantity into the mouth of the miserable *Vroucolacas*.

"For our part, we kept impressing upon the Magistrates of the town that in such circumstances it was their duty as pious Christian folk to appoint a special watch all night long in order to see what took place in the streets; and owing to this precaution at last they caught a number of beggars and other vagabonds who most certainly had been responsible for a good deal of the disorder and bother. This is not to say that they originated it, or that they were even mainly to blame for the turmoil and disturbances. Yet they had some small part in the panic, and apparently these ruffians were released from prison a great deal too soon, for two days afterwards in order to make up for the hard fare which had been their lot whilst they were in jail, they once more began to empty the jars of wine of those who were foolish enough to leave their houses empty and unguarded all night long without any sort of protection. Nevertheless the inhabitants placed their faith in prayers and religious observances.

"One day as they were chanting certain litanies, after they had pierced with a large number of naked swords the grave of the dead body, which they used to exhume three or four times a day merely to satisfy an idle curiosity, an Albanian who happened just then to be visiting Myconos took upon himself to say in a tone of the most absolute authority that in a case like this it was to the last degree ridiculous to make use of the swords of Christians. "Can you not see, poor blind buzzards that you are, that the handles of these swords, being made like a cross, prevents the devil from issuing out of the body? Why do you not rather employ Ottoman scimeters?" The advice of this learned man had no effect at all; the *Vroucolacas* was incorrigible, and all the inhabitants were thrown into the utmost consternation. They were at their wits end to know what Saint to invoke, when suddenly, just as if some cue had been given, they began to proclaim aloud throughout the whole town that the situation was intolerable; that the only way left was to burn the *Vroucolacas* whole and entire; and after that was done let the devil possess the body if he could; that it was better to adopt these extremest measures than to have the island entirely deserted. For, indeed, already some important families had begun to pack their goods and chattels with the intention of definitely withdrawing to Syra or to Tanos. The Magistrates therefore gave orders that the *Vroucolacas* should be conveyed to the point of the island of S. George, where they had prepared a great pyre with pitch and tar, lest that the wood, bone-dry as it was, should not burn fast enough of itself. What remained of the carcass was then thrown into the flames and utterly consumed in a very few minutes. This took place on 1 January, 1701. We saw the blaze as we were sailing back from Demos, and it might justly be called a festal bonfire, since after this there were even composed a number of street songs and popular ballads mocking him and turning him into ridicule.

"Throughout the whole Archipelago there is no Orthodox Greek who does not firmly believe that the devil is able to re-energize and re-vitalize dead bodies. The inhabitants of the island of Santorini in particular, have the utmost dread of this kind of werewolf (ces sortes de loupsgarous). The people of Myconos after their present fears had been dissipated expressed the utmost apprehension of the consequences which might follow such proceedings should the matter come to the knowledge of the Turkish authorities or to the ears of the Bishop of Tenos. Indeed, not a single priest would consent to go to S. George when they burned the body. The clergy were afraid that the Bishop might fine them a round sum of money for having suffered a body to be disinterred and cremated without his express sanction. As for the Turks, it is quite certain that, if they caught wind of it, the next time they visited the island they would make the whole community pay dearly for the blood of this poor wretch who had become the dread and the abomination of the whole countryside."

THE VAMPIRE
OF BLOW

A herdsman of the village of Blow (or Balu), near the Bohemian town Kadam, was a vampire who appeared to several persons, all of whom died after a passing of eight days. Unable to tolerate any more deaths, the villagers exhumed the body and impaled it with a stake. But this was one instance when the stake proved ineffective. Laughing, the vampire thanked his executioners for giving him a weapon with which to fight off dogs. That night, by his own power, the vampire pulled the stake from his heart and persisted in his hauntings, resulting in more horror and death.

Eventually the monster was placed under the wrath of the hangman. This executioner was to burn the vampire outside the town. During the transporting of the corpse it twisted about and made horrible noises. To quiet the monster another stake was driven through the heart, followed by a scream and the eruption of fresh blood. Finally the vampire body was cremated, ending his reign of horror forever.

The account, along with several others, appeared in *Magia posthuma*, by Charles Ferdinand de Schertz. The text was printed at Olmutz in 1706.

PETER PLOGOJOWITZ

In the 1738 edition of *Lettres Juives*, letter cxxxvii, by the Marquis d'
Argens, we find the observations of a foreigner as to the existence of
vampires. The case of Peter Plogojowitz, who died in September, 1728,
was sworn to by two officers of Belgrade's tribunal, and by a commanding officer of the imperial army at Gradiska, when they examined the
matter in 1725. The account is also given in Georg Conrad Hurst's
Zauber-Bibliothek, volume 1, 1821.

The account given by Raufft is as follows:

"Peter Plogojowitz, an inhabitant of a village in Hungary called
Kisolova, who, after he had been buried more than ten years, appeared
by night to several persons in the village, while they were asleep, and
squeezed their throats in such a manner that they expired within twenty-
four hours. There died in this way no less than nine persons in eight
days; and the widow of this Plogojowitz deposed that she herself had
been visited by him since his death, and that his errand was to demand
his shoes; which frightened her so much that she at once left Kisolova
and went to live somewhere else.

"These circumstances determined the inhabitants of the village to
dig up the body of Plogojowitz and burn it, in order to put a stop to
such troublesome visits. Accordingly they applied to the commanding
officer of the Emperor's troops in the district of Gradisca, in the kingdom of Hungary, and to the incumbent of the place, for leave to dig up
the corpse. They both made a great many scruples about granting it;
but the peasants declared plainly that if they were not permitted to dig
up this accursed carcase, which they were fully convinced was a vampire
they would be forced to leave the village and settle where they could.

"The officer who gave this account, seeing that there was no hin-
dering them either by fair means or foul, came in person, accompanied
by the minister of Gradisca, to Kisolova, and they were both present at
the digging up of the corpse, which they found to be free from any bad
smell, and perfectly sound, as if it had been alive, except that the tip of
the nose was a little dry and withered. The beard and hair were grown
fresh and a new set of nails had sprung up in the room of the old ones
that had fallen off. Under the former skin, which looked pale and dead,
there appeared a new one, of a natural fresh colour; and the hands and
feet were as entire as if they belonged to a person in perfect health. They

observed also that the mouth of the vampire was full of fresh blood, which the people were persuaded had been sucked by him from the persons he had killed.

"The officer and the divine having diligently examined into all the circumstances, the people, being fired with fresh indignation, and growing more fully pursuaded that this carcase was the real cause of the death of their countrymen, ran immediately to fetch a sharp stake, which being driven into his breast, there issued from the wound, and also from his nose and mouth, a great quantity of fresh, ruddy blood; and something which indicated a sort of life, was observed to come from him. The peasants then laid the body upon a pile of wood, and burnt it to ashes."

ARNOLD PAUL

One of the most authenticated and famous accounts of vampirism is the history of Arnold Paul (or Arnod Paole). Two versions of the case present their own details.

The first recounting was signed at Meduegna, near Belgrade, on 7 June 1732, by three regimental surgeons, the lieutenant-colonel, and the sub-lieutenant, and was the version recounted by Montague Summers in his book *The Vampire in Europe* published by University Books, Inc.

"In the spring of 1727 there returned from the Levant to the village of Meduegna, near Belgrade, one Arnod Paole, who in a few years' military service and varied adventure, had amassed enough to purchase a cottage and an acre or two of land in his native place, where he gave out that he meant to pass the remainder of his days. He kept his word. Arnod had yet scarcely reached the prime of manhood; and though he must have encountered the rough as well as the smooth of life, and have mingled with many a wild and reckless companion, yet his natural good disposition and honest principles had preserved him unscathed in the scenes he had passed through. At all events, such were the thoughts expressed by his neighbours as they discussed his return and settlement among them in the stube of the village hof. Nor did the frank and open countenance of Arnod, his obliging habits and steady conduct, argue their judgements incorrect. Nevertheless, there was something occasionably noticeable in his ways, a look and tone that betrayed inward disquiet. He would often refuse to join his friends, or on some sudden pleas abruptly quit their society. And he still more unaccountably, and it seemed systematically, avoided meeting his pretty neighbour, Nina, whose father occupied the next farm to his own. At the age of seventeen Nina was as charming as a picture of youth, cheerfulness, innocence, and confidence as you could have seen in all the world. You could not look into her limpid eye, which steadily returned your gaze, without seeing to the bottom of the pure and transparent spring of her thoughts. Why then did Arnod shrink from meeting her? He was young; had a little property; had health and industry; and he had told his friends he had formed no ties in other lands. Why then did he avoid the fascination of the pretty Nina, who seemed a being made to chase from any brow the clouds of gathering care? But he did so, yet less and less resolutely, for he felt the charm of her presence. Who could have done otherwise? And how long he resisted the impulse of his fondness for the innocent girl who sought to cheer his fits of depression!

"And they were to be united—were betrothed; yet still the anxious gloom would fitfully overcast his countenance, even in the sunshine of those hours.

"'What is it, dear Arnod, that makes you sad? It cannot be on my account, I know, for you were sad before you noticed me; and that, I think surely, first made me notice you.'

"'Nina,' he answered, 'I have done, I fear, a great wrong in trying to gain your affections. Nina, I have fixed impression that I shall not live; yet, knowing this, I have selfishly made my existence necessary to your happiness.'

"'How strangely you talk, dear Arnod! Who in the village is stronger and healthier than you? You feared no danger when you were a soldier. What danger do you fear as a villager of Meduegne?'

"It haunts me, Nina."

"But, Arnod, you were sad before you thought of me. Did you then fear to die?"

"Oh, Nina, it is something worse than death." And his vigorous frame shook with agony,

"Arnod, I conjure you, tell me."

"It was in Cossova this fate befell me. Here you have hitherto escaped the terrible scourge. But there they die, and the dead visit the living. I experienced the first frightful visitation, and I fled; but not till I had sought his grave and executed the dread expiation from the vampire."

"Nina's blood ran cold. She stood horror-stricken. But her young heart soon mastered her first despair. With a touching voice she spoke: 'Fear not, dear Arnod; fear not now. I will be your shield, or I will die with you!"

"And she encircled his neck with her gentle arms, and returning hope shone, Iris-like, amid her falling tears. Afterwards they found a reasonable ground for banishing or allaying their apprehension in the lengthy time which had elapsed since Arnod left Cossova, during which no fearful visitant had again approached him; and they fondly protested *that* gave them security.

"One day about a week after this conversation Arnod missed his footing when on the top of a loaded hay-wagon, and fell from it to the ground. He was picked up insensible, and carried home, where, after lingering a short time, he died. His interment, as usual, followed immediately. His fate was sad and premature. But what pencil could paint Nina's grief?

"Twenty or thirty days after his decease, several in the neighbourhood complained that they were haunted by the deceased Arnod; and what was more to the purpose, four of them died. The evil looked at sceptically was bad enough, but aggravated by the suggestions of superstition it spread a panic through the whole district. To allay the popular terror, and, if possible, to get at the root of the evil, a determination was come to publicly to disinter the body of Arnod, with the view of ascertaining whether he really was a vampire, and, in that event, of treating him conformably. The day fixed for these proceedings was the fortieth after his burial.

"It was on a grey morning in early August that the commission visited the cemetery at Meduegna, which, surrounded with a wall of stone, lies sheltered by the mountain that, rising in undulating green slopes, irregularly planted with fruit-trees, ends in an abrupt craggy ridge, covered with underwood. The graves were, for the most part, neatly kept, with borders of box, or something like it, and flowers between, and at the head of most, a small wooden cross, painted black, bearing the name of the tenant. Here and there a stone had been raised. One of terrible height, a single narrow slab, ornamented with grotesque Gothic carvings, dominated over the rest. Near this lay the grave of Arnod Paole, towards which the party moved. The work of throwing out the earth was begun by the grey, careful old sexton, who lived in the Leichenhaus beyond the great crucifix. Near the grave stood two military surgeons or *feldscherers* from Belgrade, and a drummer-boy, who held their case of instruments. The boy looked on with keen interest;

and when the coffin was exposed and rather roughly drawn out of the grave, his pale face and bright, intent eye showed how the scene moved him. The sexton lifted the lid of the coffin; the body had become inclined to one side. Then, turning it straight: 'Ha, ha! What? Your mouth not wiped since last night's work?'

"The spectators shuddered; the drummer-boy sank forward, fainting, and upset the instrument case, scattering its contents; the senior surgeon, infected with the horror of the scene, repressed a hasty exclamation. They threw water on the drummer-boy and he recovered, but would not leave the spot. Then they inspected the body of Arnod. It looked as if it had not been dead a day. After handling it, the scarfskin came off, but below were *new skin* and *new nails*! How could they have come there but from this foul feeding? The case was clear enough: there lay before them the thing they dreaded—the vampire! So, without more ado, they simply drove a stake through poor Arnod's chest, whereupon a quantity of blood gushed forth, and the corpse uttered a dreadful groan.

"'Murder! Murder!' shrieked the drummer-boy, as he rushed wildly, with convulsed gestures, from the scene."

More corpses were unearthed in the vampire condition five years later. All were as if newly buried, with new nails and flesh growing beneath the loose scarfskin. Some of the examples were 1) Miliza, a woman having died of a three-month illness, and buried a hundred days; 2) Stana, who during life admitted she anointed herself with vampire blood to ward off one of the monsters, died after three days of sickness and was buried for three months; 3) Joachim, a teenager buried for ninety days; 4) Ruscha, a woman dead from a ten-day illness, and buried for a month and a half; 5) Rhade, a servant sick for three months and buried for five weeks; 6) Stanko, a heyduk dead for six weeks; 7) Millak, a young heyduk, buried for six weeks; 8) Stanjoika, a heyduk's wife, buried fourteen days; 9) an eight year-old child buried for ninety days; 10) a ten year-old girl buried two months, discovered with blood in her chest; and 11) the sixteen year-old son of the heyduk Milloc, buried nine weeks. The wife of a man named Hadnuck, buried seven weeks, and her baby buried twenty-one days, had decayed in the normal fashion, so that the vampire state could not be attributed to peculiarities in the soil.

The second version of the account was noted by Dom Augustin Calmet in his *Dissertation on Vampires*.

"In the part of Hungary, known in Latin by the name of *Oppida*

Heidonum, on the other side of the Tibiscus, vulgarly called the Teyss;
that is between that part of this river which waters the happy country of
Tockay, and the frontiers of Transylvania, the people named *Heydukes*
have a notion that there are dead persons, called by them *vampires*,
which suck the blood of the living, so as to make them fall away visibly
to skin and bones, while the carcasses themselves, like leeches, are filled
with blood to such a degree that it comes out of all the apertures of
their body. This notion has lately been confirmed by several facts, which
I think we cannot deny the truth of, considering the witnesses who
attest them. Some of the most considerable of these facts I shall now
relate.

"About five years ago, an Heyduke named Arnold Paul, an inhabitant of Medreiga, was killed by a cart full of hay that fell upon him.
About thirty days after his death, four persons died suddenly, with all
the symptoms usually attending, those who are killed by *vampires*. It
was then remembered that this Arnold Paul had frequently told a story
of his having been tormented by a Turkish *vampire*, in the
neighbourhood of Cassova, upon the borders of the Turkish Servia (for
the notion is that those who have been passive *vampires* in their lifetime become active ones after death; or, in other words, that those who
have had their blood sucked become suckers in their turn) but that he
had been cured by eating some of the earth upon the vampire's grave,
and by rubbing himself with his blood. This precaution, however, did
not hinder him from being guilty himself after his death; for, upon
digging up his corpse forty days after his burial, he was found to have
all the marks of an arch-vampire. His body was fresh and ruddy, his
hair, beard, and nails were grown, and his veins were full of fluid blood,
which ran from all parts of his body upon the shroud that he was
buried in. The *hadnagy*, or baliff of the village, who was present at the
digging up of the corpse, and was very expert in the whole business of
vampirism, ordered a sharp stake to be drove through the body of the
deceased, and to let it pass through his heart, which was attended with
a hideous cry from the carcass, as if it had been alive. This ceremony
being performed, they cut off the head, and burnt the body to ashes.
After this, they proceeded in the same manner with the four other
persons that died of vampirism, lest they also should be troublesome.
But all these executions, could not hinder this dreadful prodigy from
appearing again last year, at the distance of five years from its first
breaking out. In the space of three months, seventeen persons of different ages and sexes died of vampirism, some without any previous ill-

ness, and others after languishing two or three days. Among others, it was said, that a girl, named Stanoska, daughter of the Heyduke Jotuitzo, went to bed in perfect health, but awoke in the middle of the night, trembling, crying out that the son of the Heyduke Millo, who died about nine weeks before, had almost strangled her while she was asleep. From that time she fell into a languishing state, and died at three days' end. Her evidence against Millo's son was looked upon as proof of his being a *vampire*, and, upon digging up his body, he was found to be such.

"At a consultation of the principal inhabitants of the place, attended by physicians and chirurgeons, it was considered how it was possible that the plague should break out afresh, after the precautions that had been taken some years before: and, at last, it was found out that the original offender, Arnold Paul, had not only destroyed the four persons mentioned above, but had killed several beasts, which the late *vampires*, and particularly the son of Millo, had fed upon. Upon this foundation a resolution was taken to dig up all the persons that had died within a certain time. Out of forty were found seventeen, with all the evident tokens of vampirism; and they had all stakes drove through their hearts, their heads cut off, their bodies burnt, and their ashes thrown into the river.

"All these several enquiries and executions were carried on with all the forms of the law, and attested by several officers who were in garrison in that country, by the chirurgeon-majora of the regiments, and by the principal inhabitants of the place. The original papers were all sent, in January last, to the Imperial council of war at Vienna, which had issued out a commission to several officers, to enquire into the truth of the fact.

Patriarchal Vampires

Certain species of vampire tended to favor members of their own families as victims. In Dom Augustin Calmet's *Dissertation on Vampires* he related the following well authenticated case:

"It is now about fifteen years since a soldier, who was quartered in the house of a Haidamack peasant, upon the frontiers of Hungary, saw, as he was at the table with his landlord, a stranger come and sit down by them. The master of the house and the rest of the company were strangely terrified, but the soldier knew not what to make of it. The next day the peasant died, and, upon the soldier's enquiring into the meaning of it, he was told that it was the landlord's father, who had been dead and buried above ten years, that came and sat down at table, and gave his son notice of his death.

"The soldier soon propagated the story through his regiment, and by this means it reached the general officers, who commissioned the count de Cabreras, a captain in Alandetti's regiment of foot, to make an exact enquiry into the fact. The count, attended by several officers, a surgeon, and a notary, came to the house, and took the deposition of all the family, who unanimously swore that the spectre was the landlord's father, and that all the soldier had said was strictly true. The same was also attested by all inhabitants of the village.

"In consequence of this the body of the spectre was dug up, and found to be in the same state as if it has been but just dead, the blood like that of a living person. The count de Cabreras ordered its head to be cut off, and the corpse to be buried again. He then proceeded to take depositions against other spectres of the same sort, and particularly against a man who had been dead above thirty years, and had made his appearance three several times in his own house at meal-time. At his first visit he had fastened upon the neck of his own brother, and sucked his blood; at his second, he had treated one of his children in the same manner; and the third time, he fastened upon a servant of the family, and all three died upon the spot.

"Upon this evidence, the count gave orders that he should be dug up, and being found, like the first, with his blood in a fluid state, as if he had been alive, a great nail was drove through his temples, and he was buried again. The count ordered a third to be burnt, who had been dead above sixteen years, and was found guilty of murdering two of his own children by sucking their blood. The commissioner then made his report to the general officers, who sent a deputation to the emperor's court, consisting of officers, lawyers, physicians, chirurgeons, and some divines, to go and enquire into the cause of these extraordinary events, upon the spot.

"The gentleman who acquainted me with all these particulars, had them from the count de Cabreras himself, at Fribourg in Brisgau, in the year 1730.

"In the village of Kisilova, three leagues from Grandisch, an old man of 62 died in September; three days after the funeral he appeared before his son in the night and asked for food. His son gave him some and he disappeared. The next day the son told his neighbours what had happened. That night the old man did not appear; but the following night he appeared and demanded food: no one knows whether his son gave it to him or not, but in the morning the son was found dead in his bed, and on that same day five or six others in the village suddenly fell ill, and they died one after the other a few days later. The governor of the district forwarded a report to the Tribunal in Belgrade, and they sent off two officials and an executioner to deal with the matter. The governor who first reported it travelled from Grandisch to see with his own eyes what had happened. All the bodies that had been buried for the last six weeks were disinterred; when they reached the body of the old man, they found his eyes were open and of a red colour, and the respiration was normal, though he was still quite still and dead. From this they concluded that he was an undoubted vampire. The hangman drove a stake through the heart. A great fire was made, and the corpse was reduced to ashes. It is said that 'none of the marks of vampirism was found on the body of the son, nor on any of the others.'"

Christopher Lee (with Leonora Ruffo) as a vampire in the film, "Hercules in the Haunted World." Copyright 1961, Warner Brothers.

STEPHEN HUBNER, VAMPIRE OF TREAUTENAU

Stephen Hubner returned from death as a human vampire. From the years 1730–1732 he haunted the Slavic town of Treautenau by attacking both people and cattle.

The official reports said that the monster delighted in strangling his victims, a common method of murder by vampires.

Upon orders given by the supreme court of the district, the corpse of Stephen Hubner was exhumed. Buried five months the body was found to be in the vampire state, free from decay.

Taken to the public gallows, the corpse was decapitated by the official executioner. Then the remains were cremated, the ashes mingling with the wind.

Although not disinterred in the vampire condition, the corpses buried near Hubner were burned with religious sanction and many prayers, then returned with reverence to their graves.

THE GIANT VAMPIRE OF CHINA

A particularly haunted Chinese temple of the legendary heroes Kwan Yu, Liu Pei, and Chang Fei was so feared that even the priest would not remain there, opening it by day only during the sacrifices of spring and autumn. On a particular night of 1741 a shepherd asked for permission to sleep the night in the temple, while his flock waited under the verandah. Despite the warnings of the priest he dared enter the building, armed with but a candle and a whip. His only company was the trio of statues in the likenesses of Kwan Yu, Liu Pei, and Chang Fei. Yet the shepherd could not escape the feeling that the temple was infested by some unnatural presence.

A noise aroused him at midnight, issuing from the pedestal beneath the statues. The shepherd turned immediately toward the origin of the sound and witnessed the appearance of a giant with great claws and a fleece of green. Its breath smelled like a rotting corpse. Without warning the giant attacked. But the shepherd evaded those talons by expertly wielding the whip. As the monster seemed impervious to the whip the shepherd fled from the temple.

The following day, after relating the event to the people, the shepherd returned to investigate the pedestal from which the greenish vampire emerged. Again the temple was empty. But when a weird mist drifted from the cracked stone, the phenomenon was reported to the magistrate who gave permission for the disruption of the pedestal. The people dug below the stone where a giant man, dried like a mummy and fitting the description given by the shepherd, was discovered. They built a funeral pyre next to the temple, carried out the green covered corpse, and cremated it. As the fire ate away the fleecy epidermis the creature screeched, while new blood splashed from the burning carcass.

After the giant vampire had been entirely consumed by the cleansing fires, that temple of China was free from the monster's visitations.

SOME VAMPIRES RECORDED BY DOM CALMET

Augustin Calmet related many vampiric occurrences in his writings. The following are typical:

"I have heard from the late Monsieur de Vassimont, Chief Financial Advisor in Bar, that when he was sent to Moravia by the late Duke Leopold of Lorraine to mind the affairs of his brother, Monseigneur Prince Charles, Bishop of Olmutz and Osnaburgh, he was told it was common knowledge in these parts that a man, dead for some time past, might suddenly make an appearance at a meal and sit down among his friends without a word, nodding his head perhaps at one of the company, who would then invariably sicken and die a few days later. This occurrence was confirmed by several persons, among them a priest who had seen it happen more than once.

"The bishops and priests to the country consulted Rome about these singular occurrences, but they received no reply, for it was held that they were delusions or popular superstitions. Later they were advised to exhume the bodies of the men who haunted them and to burn them, or destroy them in some other manner. Thus they were delivered from the importunities of the apparitions, which are now much less common in these parts; so said the priest.

"A little book has been written about these apparitions entitled *Magia Posthuma*, by Charles Ferdinand de Schertz, printed at Olmutz in 1706 and dedicated to Prince Charles of Lorraine, Bishop of Olmutz and Osnaburgh. The author relates that in a certain village a woman was buried in the cemetery in the normal manner, after receiving the sacraments at her death. Four days later, the villagers heard a great uproar and clamouring, and many of them saw an apparition which first took the form of a dog and then of a man: striking them, catching them by the throat, squeezing them in the stomach till they nearly suffocated; they were bruised all over and reduced to a pitiable condition, pale, thin and exhausted. The apparition attacked animals as well, and cows were discovered bruised and half-dead; sometimes they would be tied together by the tail. The horses would be found lying as though they were weak from exhaustion, heated, sweating, and gasping, covered with lather as though they had run a hard race. These calamities lasted for several months.

"The following is a letter written to an acquaintance of mine regarding the apparitions of Hungary:

"'In response to the questions of Monsieur l'Abbe Dom Calmet regarding vampires, the author has the honour to assure him that there is nothing more true and indisputable than the accounts that he has doubtless read in the published gazettes of every European country; but as well as these public records Monsieur l'Abbe must consider the indisputable evidence of the deputation of Belgrade, ordered by his late Imperial Majesty Charles VI, of glorious memory, and directed by his late Serene Highness, Duke Charles Alexander of Wurtemburgh, then vice-regent or governor of the kingdom of Serbia; but I cannot at the present moment cite the year, the month, or the date without my papers, which are not with me at the moment.

"'The Prince sent a deputation from Belgrade consisting of both civil and military officials, with the Public Prosecutor of the kingdom, to a village where a notorious vampire, dead many years since, was ravaging his kinsmen; for it is notable that the bloodsuckers only seek to destroy their own families. This deputation was composed of respected persons, both civil and military, well known for their experience and respectability; they were put on oath, and accompanied by a lieutenant of the Grenadiers of Prince Alexander of Wurtemburg's regiment and twenty-four of his men.

"'Many reputable citizens accompanied the deputation, even the Duke himself, who happened to be in Belgrade at the time, in order to have visible proof of the strange occurrences.

"'When they reached the village they discovered that the vampire had already dispatched three of his nieces and nephews and one of his own brothers within the past fortnight. He had just commenced on his fifth victim, his young and beautiful niece, and had sucked blood twice when the tragedy was arrested in the following manner.

"'At dusk some members of the deputation went to the grave in the presence of a crowd of people. My informant was unable to tell me precisely at what time the previous victims were sucked nor the details. The pangs are so violent that after his blood has been sucked the victim remains in a pitiful state of weakness and lassitude. The vampire had been buried three years ago; now they saw a light over his tomb like a flickering lamp.

"'The grave was opened and a man was revealed, as whole and apparently as healthy as anyone present; his hair, and the hair of his body, his nails, teeth and eyes (which were half-open) were all firmly attached as in life, and his heart was beating.

"'He was taken from his coffin; the body was not truly flexibile, but no particle of bone or flesh was missing; his heart was then pierced through with a species of sharp iron bar: a whitish fluid issued, mixed with blood, but the blood predominating, and the whole without any bad odour; next the head was cut off with a sort of axe such as is used in England for executions: the same fluid and blood issued as before, but more abundantly.

"'The body was put into the ground, covered with quicklime to consume it as rapidly as possible, and from this time onwards the girl who had been sucked twice be an to recover. A bluish patch forms on the spot where these people have been sucked; but the spot is not precise, it shows in different places at different times.'

"On 17th October, 1746, a kinsman of the same officer wrote to me that his brother, who had spent twenty years in Hungary and was well acquainted with the local beliefs about ghosts, acknowledged that these people were exceptionally credulous and superstitious and ascribed all their misfortunes to witchcraft; that the moment they suspected that one of the dead was bewitching them they submitted the matter to the magistrate, and if a few witnesses could be found to testify, he would open the grave; the corpse would be decapitated with a spade and if the least drop of blood were found, they would conclude that it must have been sucked from the sick person. But my correspondent does not seem to be swayed by these local superstitions."

Vampire Viscount
of France

Due to the image of the vampire popularized by literature and motion pictures, the Undead is usually associated with wealth and nobility. Miss Jessie Adelaide Middleton in her *Another Grey Ghost Book* tells of a titled vampire as vicious as Count Dracula himself:

"A French viscount—de Morieve by name—was one of the very few French noblemen who managed to retain their estates through the troublesome times of the French Revolution. He was an extraordinary looking man, very tall and thin, with a high, almost pointed forehead, and protruding teeth.

"Under an air of suave courtesy and kindness he concealed a ferociously cruel disposition, which showed itself when the fires of the great revolution had burned themselves out, and all was once more quiet. To get level, as it were, with the working classes, he sent for his retainers and workpeople one by one, and, after he had interviewed them, cut off their heads. It is not surprising to hear that, in return, he himself met death by assassination at the hands of some of the peasantry.

"No sooner, however, was the viscount laid in the grave than an appalling number of young children died in the neighbourhood, all of whom bore the vampire marks at the throat. Later on, when he had been buried for some time, and while the tomb was being repaired, there were nine more cases in a single week. The awful slaughter went on until seventy-two years passed away, and the viscount's grandson succeeded to the title.

"Young de Morieve, hearing the appalling stories of his grandfather, consulted a priest with the idea of laying his horrible ancestor's ghost, and, after some discussion and delay, it was decided to open the tomb. The services of a man specially successful in such cases were obtained, and the vault was opened in the presence of the authorities.

"Every coffin was found to have undergone the usual process of rotting away, except that of the old viscount, which, after seventy-two years, was perfectly strong and sound. The lid was removed and the body was found quite fresh and free from decomposition. The face was flushed and there was blood in the heart and chest. The skin was soft and natural. New nails had grown on both hands and feet.

"The body was removed from the coffin and a white thorn was

driven by the expert through the heart of the corpse, with the ghastly result that blood and water poured forth and the corpse groaned and screamed. Then the remains were burned on the seashore; and from that day the child-deaths ceased and there were no more mysterious crimes in the neighbourhood.

"The family archives were searched and it was found that the old viscount had come originally from Persia, where he married an Indian wife, and afterwards took up his residence in France, where he became a naturalised subject. The vampire taint was in his blood."

A Russian Vampire

An eye witness told the following vampire history to Madame Blavatsky, who recorded it in her classic *Isis Unveiled:*

"About the beginning of the present century, there occurred in Russia, one of the more frightful cases of Vampirism on record. The governor of the Province Tch was a man of about sixty years, of a malicious, tyrannical, cruel, and jealous disposition. Clothed with despotic authority, he exercised without stint, as his brutal instincts prompted. He fell in love with the pretty daughter of a subordinate official. Although the girl was betrothed to a young man whom she loved, the tyrant forced her father to consent to his having her marry him; and the poor victim, despite her despair, became his wife. His jealous disposition exhibited itself. He beat her, confined her to her room for weeks together, and prevented her from seeing anyone except in his presence. He finally fell sick and died. Finding his end approaching, he made her swear never to marry again; and with fearful oaths threatened that, in case she did, he would return from his grave and kill her. He was buried in the cemetery across the river, and the young widow experienced no further annoyance, until, nature getting the better of her fears, she listened to the importunities of her former lover, and they were again betrothed.

"On the night of the customary betrothal-feast, when all had returned, the old mansion was aroused by shrieks proceeding from her room. The doors were burst open and the unhappy woman was found lying on her bed in swoon. At the same time, a carriage was heard rumbling out of the courtyard. Her body was found to be black and blue in places, as from the effect of pinches, and from a slight puncture on her neck drops of blood were oozing. Upon recovering she stated that her deceased husband had suddenly entered her room, appearing exactly as in life, with the exception of a dreadful pallor; that he had upbraided her for her inconstancy, and then beaten and pinched her most cruelly. Her story was disbelieved; but the next morning the guard stationed at the other end of the bridge which spans the river, reported that, just before midnight, a black coach and six had driven furiously past them, towards the town, without answering their challenge.

"The new governor, who disbelieved the story of the apparition, took nevertheless the precaution of doubling the guards across the bridge. The same thing happened, however, night after night; the soldiers declaring that the toll-bar at their station near the bridge would rise of itself, and the special equipage sweep by them despite their efforts to stop it. At the same time every night the coach would rumble into the courtyard of the house; the watchers, including the widow's family, and the servants would be thrown into a heavy sleep, and every morning the young victims would be found bruised, bleeding and swooning as before. The town was thrown into consternation. The physicians had no explanation to offer; priests came to pass the night in prayer, but as midnight approached, all would be seized with the terrible lethargy. Finally, the archbishop of the province came, and performed the ceremony of exorcism in person, but the following morning the governor's widow was found worse than ever. She was now brought to death's door.

"The governor was now driven to take the severest measures to stop the ever-increasing panic in the town. He stationed fifty Cossacks along the bridge, with orders to stop the spectre carriage at all hazards. Promptly at the usual hour, it was heard and seen approaching from the direction of the cemetery. The officer of the guard, and a priest bearing a crucifix, planted themselves in front of the toll-bar, and together shouted: "In the name of God and the Czar, who goes there?" Out of the coach window was thrust a well-remembered head, and a familiar voice responded: "The Privy Councillor of State and Governor C—!" At the same moment, the Officer, the priest, and the soldiers were flung aside as by an electric shock, and the ghostly equipage passed by them, before they could recover breath.

"The archbishop then resolved as a last expedient to resort to the time-honoured plan of exhuming the body, and pinning it to the earth with an oaken stake driven through its heart. This was done with great religious ceremony in the presence of the whole populace. The story is that the body was found gorged with blood, and with red cheeks and lips. At the instant that the first blow was struck upon the stake, a groan issued from the corpse, and a jet of blood spurted high in the air. The archbishop pronounced the usual exorcism, the body re-interred, and from that time no more was heard of the Vampire."

Two Vrukolakas of Grevena

William Martin Leake in his *Travels in Northern Greece*, volume IV, chapter xxxviii, published in 1835, related the following:

"It would be difficult now to meet with an example of the most barbarous of all those superstitions, that of the Vrukolaka. The name being Illyric, seems to acquit the Greeks of the invention, which was probably introduced into the country by the barbarians of the Slavonic race. Tournefort's description is admitted to be correct. The Devil is supposed to enter the Vrukolaka, who, rising from the grave, torments first his nearest relations, and then others, causing their death or loss of health. The remedy is to dig up the body, and if after it has been exorcized by the priest, the demon still persists in annoying the living, to cut the body into small pieces, or if that be not sufficient, to burn it. The metropolitan Bishop of Larissa lately informed me, that when metropolitan of Greneva, he once received advice of a papas having disinterred two bodies, and thrown them into the Haliacmon, on pretence of their being Vrukolakas. Upon being summoned before the bishop, the priest confessed the fact, and asserted in justification, that a report prevailed of a large animal having been seen to issue, accompanied with flames, out of the grave in which the two bodies had been buried. The bishop began by obliging the priest to pay him 250 piastres (his holiness did not add that he made over the money to the poor). He then sent for scissors to cut off the priest's beard, but was satisfied with frightening him. By then publishing throughout the diocese, that any similar offense would be punished with double the fine and certain loss of station, the bishop effectually quieted all the vampires of his episcopal province."

VAMPIRES
ACCORDING TO LAWSON

J. C. Lawson placed the following observation of vampirism in his work *Modern Greek Folklore:*

"Nowadays, on the contrary, the presents of food to the dead are generally continued up to the third anniversary, when exhumation takes place. Then, if the evidence of men's eyes assures them that dissolution has been fully effected—that the body is gone and only the white bones remain—there is no further thought of provision for the dead; but in the rare cases in which the disintegration of the corpse is not yet complete, the relatives are not freed from their obligations. I witnessed a remarkable case of this kind at Leonidi on the east coast of Laconia. The two graves had just been opened when I arrived, and the utmost anxiety prevailed because in both cases there was only partial decomposition—in one case so little that the general outline of the features could be made out—and it was feared that one or both of the dead persons had become *vrykolakas*. The remains, when I saw them had been removed to the chapel attached to the burial ground. Meanwhile the question was debated as to what should be done with them. Dissolution must be affected both in the interests of the dead themselves and in those of the whole community. Extraordinary measures were required. The best measure—I am reporting what I actually heard the best measure next to prayer (which had been tried without effect) was to burn the remains, and the bolder spirits of the village counselled this plan; but this would have been a breach of law and order, and the authorities of the place would have none of it. The priest proposed re-interment; but here the relatives objected. They had had trouble enough and expense enough; they had kept the 'unsleeping lamp' burning at the grave, and had provided all the memorial feasts; they would not consent to re-inter the body and to be at the same charge for an indefinite time, without knowing when the corpse might be properly 'loosed' and their tendence of it over. They would find some way of dissolving it, and that speedily.

"And so indeed they did; and I, for a short time, was a spectator of the scene. On the floor of the chapel there were two large baskets containing the remains; there were men seated beside them busy with knives; and there were women kneeling at wash-tubs and scouring the bones that were handed to them with soap and soda. The work continued for two days. At the end of that time the bones were shown white and clean. All else had disappeared—and probably been burnt in secret, but the secret was kept close. It was therefore claimed and allowed that dissolution was complete.

"The attitude adopted by the relatives on this occasion makes it perfectly clear that all the care expended on the dead is obligatory up to the time of dissolution, but no longer. So long as the fleshy substance remains in this world, provision of food must be made for it; when it has disappeared and only the bones are left, the departed cease to be dependent upon their surviving relatives, and no further anxiety is felt for their welfare."

UNCLE HELLEBORUS AND MR. TULIP

Dr. Franz Hartmann recorded the following case of spiritual vampirism, involving a psychic bond between two people, under the title "A Modem Case of Vampirism":

"In the night of 31 December, 1888, Mr. and Mrs. Rose (the names in this history are pseudonyms, but the facts are true) went to bed as poor people and on the morning of 1 January, 1889, they woke up finding themselves rich. An uncle to whom they owed their poverty because he kept them from coming into the legal possession of their rightful property, had died during the night. There are some occurrences of an occult character, connected with this event, which will be interesting to those who wish to find practical proofs and demonstrations in their investigations of the 'night side of nature'.

"Mr. Rose is a young, but very cleaver, professional man in this city, who being at the beginning of his career has, therefore, only an exceedingly limited number of clients. His young wife is one of the most amiable ladies whom it has been my good fortune to meet; a spiritually minded woman and more of a poetess than an economist. She had been brought up under the most affluent circumstances, her father being very rich, and she was the only and therefore the pet child in her luxurious home. It would be too complicated a task to tell how it happened that the property which she inherited fell first into the hands of her uncle, a spiteful and avaricious man. Sufficient to say that this man, whom we will call Helleborus, had by his intrigues and law-suits managed to keep Mrs. Rose's property in his hands; giving her and her husband no support whatever. More than once they were forced to borrow money from their friends, in order to keep themselves from starvation.

"As 'Uncle Helleborus' was in the last stage of consumption, their only hope was that his death would soon put an end to his law-suits, and bring them into possession of what rightfully belonged to them.

"Uncle Helleborus, however, did not seem inclined to die. Year after year, he kept on coughing and expectorating; but with all this he out-lived many who predicted his death. After making to Mr. and Mrs. Rose a proposal of a settlement, which would have left him in possession of nearly all the property and given to them only a pittance, he went to Meran, last autumn, to avoid the cold climate of Vienna.

"In their embarrassing circumstances, they were much inclined to accept the settlement; but they concluded to first consult about it a friend, an eminent lawyer; and this gentlemen (whom we will call Mr. Tulip, as everybody in Vienna knows his real name) advised them to the contrary. This enraged Helleborus against Tulip, and starting into a blind rage, he swore that if he found an opportunity of killing Tulip, he would surely do so.

"Mr. Tulip was an extraordinary strong, well-built and healthy man; but at the beginning of December last, soon after Mr. Helleborus's departure for Meran, he suddenly failed in health. The doctors could not locate the disease, and he grew rapidly thinner and weaker, complaining of nothing but extreme lassitude, and feeling like a person who was daily bled. Finally, on 20 December, last, all Vienna was surprised to hear that Mr. Tulip had died. Post-mortem examination showing all the organs in perfect normal condition, the doctors found nothing better to register but death from marasmus (emaciation), as the cause of this extraordinary event. Strange to say, during the last days of the disease (if it can be so called), when his mind became flighty, he often imagined that a stranger was troubling him, and the description which he gave of that invisible personage fitted Mr. Helleborus with perfect accuracy.

"During Mr. Tulip's sickness, news came from Meran that Mr. Helleborus was rapidly gaining strength and recovering from his illness in a most miraculous manner; but there were some people who expressed grave doubts as to whether this seeming recovery would be lasting. On the day of Mr. Tulip's funeral, Mr.—, a prominent member of the Theosophical Society, now in Austria, remarked to Mrs. Rose: 'You will see that now that Mr. Tulip is dead, his Vampire will die too.'

"On 1 January, 1889, Mr. Rose dreamed that he saw Uncle Helleborus looking perfectly healthy. He expressed his surprise about it, when a voice, as if coming from a long distance said: 'Uncle Helleborus is dead.' The voice sounded a second time, and this once far more powerfully, repeating the same sentence; and this time Mr. Rose awoke with the sound of that voice still ringing in his ears, and communicated to his wife the happy news that 'Uncle Helleborus was dead.' Two hours afterwards a telegram came from Meran, announcing the demise of Uncle Helleborus, which had occurred on that very night, and calling upon Mr. Rose to come and attend to the funeral. It was found that Mr. Helleborus had begun to grow rapidly worse from the day when Mr. Tulip died.

"The only rational explanation of such cases I have found in Paracelsus."

The Vampire
of Jewett

An American newspaper, the Norwich *Courier*, in 1854 told of a vampiric incident in the neighboring town of Jewett.

Horace Ray, a resident of Griswold, died of consumption in the year 1847. His two sons followed, him with the same disease, the last and younger of the two wasting away to death in 1852. Finally a third son was destroyed by the sickness.

The family believed that it was the vampire bodies of the first two brothers that acted like parasites on the family. The only thing to do seemed to disinter the bodies and destroy them.

On 8 June 1854 the family and a group of friends marched to the cemetery and solemnly removed the corpses from their graves.

The bodies were then placed upon a funeral pyre and burned to ashes.

VAMPIRES OF
RHODE ISLAND AND CHICAGO

William Rose, a citizen of the village of Placedale, Rhode Island, believed that his daughter was a vampire who was sapping away the vitality of the members of his family.

With his own hands, Rose dug up the corpse of his daughter, cut out the heart, and burned the organ to ashes.

The incident was reported in an 1874 edition of the Providence *Journal.*

In 1875, a Dr. Dryer witnessed an occurrence in Chicago, wherein a woman dead from consumption was disinterred and cremated as a vampire who preyed upon her living relatives, causing their deaths.

EXORCISM
OF A VRYKOLAKAS

There are numerous prescribed methods to destroy vampires. Most of these are not for the squeamish, for they deal with the physical destruction of corpses.

There is, however, a method by which the vampire can be destroyed without any physical contact—the exorcism of the vampiric entity through the holy words of a priest. This method is only sometimes successful.

One particular account involved a woman who returned from the dead as a *vrykolakas.*

"The priest of the village laid on the ground one of the dead woman's shifts, over the neck of which he walked, held up by two men, for fear the vampire should seize him. While in this position he read verses from the New Testament, till the shift swelled up and split. When this rent takes place the evil spirit is supposed to escape through the opening."

The account was included by Newton in his *Travels and Discoveries in the Levant.*

Vampires Related by Sir Rennell Rodd

The *Customs and Lore of Modern Greece*, by Sir Rennell Rodd, and published by David Scott, London, in 1892, included the following vampire histories:

"And here it may be mentioned that the Vourkolakas is not invariably the blood-sucking vampire in recent tradition, but that the name is sometimes extended to include mere spectres of the departed who return to earth, and that in this sense, at any rate, the superstition is by no means extinct as Colonel Leake appears to have believed. In the memoirs of N. Nicholas Dragoumis there is an interesting account of its effect on the populace of Naxos, where early in the thirties a cholera epidemic had carried off a great number of victims. The rumour was circulated that the Naxian dead in the other world were so numerous that they overpowered Charos (the lord of the dead), and were coming back again to earth to take possession of their own. The fear of these Vourkolakas, as they call them, was so great that the inhabitants rushed to their houses at sunset, barred doors and windows, and piled furniture against them; but often in vain, for the spectres entered through the key-holes and scared the living for many an anxious day.

"The Vourkolakas is, however, generally ravenous".

Rodd proceeded to comment upon the story of the Katakhanas, the vampire of Crete, related by Robert Pashley in his *Travels in Crete* in 1827.

"Pashley's experience," said Sir Rennell Rodd, "of course, dates back a good many years, but I was myself told a story in Crete of a man well known to my informant, who had the power of fortelling when people were going to die. From time to time this man would fall ill in a mysterious manner, and his invariable explanation was that the dead whose doom he had foretold were returning as Katakhanades to torment him in various manners, though it would seem rather as ghosts of the common sort than as vampires, and in this explanation he appeared to be perfectly sincere."

VAMPIRE OF
1894 LONDON

The following case of a living vampire was published in an 1894 issue of the London police news.

"Defendant admitted he had bitten the child because he loved it."

The defendant cited was a thirty year-old man, accused of maltreating his wife's illegitimate daughter for several months. The child's eyes, lips, and hands had been bitten and sucked of blood by the man. Even the girl's pinafore was smeared with blood.

VAMPIRES RECORDED
BY HARTMANN

Dr. Franz Hartmann, in the publication *Borderland*, Volume III, 1895, related the following histories of vampirism.

A certain man who was a chronic drinker loved a woman and proposed marriage to her. Because of his major fault, she refused his hand. The man took the matter extremely hard. With a feeling of utter dejection he shot himself to death.

Shortly after his suicide, a vampire in the dead man's form began to haunt the woman with regularity. Although she could not see him, she was without doubt aware of his presence.

Medical men were called in to examine the woman but could find nothing more wrong than hysteria. Even though she took the medicines prescribed to her, the hauntings continued.

It was not until that she resorted to exorcism by a man with strong faith that the vampire entity ceased its visitations.

Another case related by Hartmann involved the servant boy of a miller. The boy had entered the service and soon became ill. His appetite increased to incredible proportions. But the more, he ate the weaker he became. When questioned about his strange condition the boy told of an invisible entity which, every midnight, lay across his chest and absorbed his vitality so that he became momentarily paralyzed and mute.

The miller desired to stop the actions of the infernal entity. Sleeping with the boy, he instructed him to give a signal when the invisible creature settled upon him. The boy did as he was instructed and told the miller that the unearthly visitor had arrived. Extending his hand,

the man touched what he could not see—an eliptically shaped forma-
tion of gelatinous substance, suggesting a constitution of ectoplasm.
Without delay the miller grasped the creature, which struggled savagely
to free itself, then hurled it into the fire. The servant boy returned to
normal health and the unseen vampire never came back.

Finally Dr. Hartmann related:

"A woman in this vicinity has a ghost, or so she calls it, a 'dual'
with whom she lives on the most intimate terms as husband and wife.
She converses with him and he makes her do the most irrational things.
He has many whims, and she being a woman of means, gratifies them.
If her dual wants to go and see Italy 'through her eyes, ' she has to go to
Italy and let him enjoy the sights. She does not care for balls and the-
atres; but her dual wants to attend them, and so she has to go. She gives
lessons to her dual and 'educates' him in the things of this world and
commits no end of follies. At the same time her dual draws all her
strength from her, and she has to vampirize every one she comes in
contact with to make up for the loss."

Andilaveris, Broukolakas of Kythnos

The island of Kythnos is, like Santorini, a place often plagued by
vampires. Among the inhabitants of Kythnos was the wide-spread belief that corpses found in a state of natural mummification are undoubtedly vampires, whereas normal decomposition is a sign of saint-
hood. Many diseases, particularly tuberculosis (formerly "consumption"),
were attributed to vampiric attacks. In M. Henry Hauttecoeur's *Le
Folklore de l'Ile de Kythnos*, published in Brussels in 1898, the following
account of a *Broukolakas* or vampire was given:

"And yet some say there are no ghosts at all nowadays because they
boast that they have found a way to prevent any ghost from appearing.
What is a ghost, indeed, but simply the devil who takes possession of a
corpse, making his entry through the dead man's mouth. Very well,
then, in order to prevent any such public misfortune there is only one
thing to be done, and that is to place in the mouth of a dead person, as
soon as he has breathed his last sigh, a little cross made out of wax. The
devil would never dare to pass over the cross. And so there are no more
ghosts who are able to appear. Yet in spite of all the panacea apparitions are still seen on the island of Kythnos, not as many perhaps as

there used to be in the good old days, but yet there are some ghosts left. Andilaveris, for instance, everybody on the island knew all about him ... he was the most vexatious. Without the slightest consideration for the high esteem in which his family and relations were so deservedly held, he unmercifully plagued the whole village. At night he came out of his grave and he used to walk up and down every street in Messaria. Sometimes he would even make his way into a house, he would sit down at table, he would eat like a hungry giant and drink like a fish, and then when he had gorged his fill of wine and swallowed all the dainties he pleased, he used to amuse himself by smashing the plates and the glasses, by clattering the pots and pans, howling horribly all the while like a mad werewolf.

"The whole place was in a state of frenzied panic; directly dusk fell the people one and all shut themselves up in their houses behind locked doors and nobody dared to set foot abroad. The women whose husbands were away used to go and sleep at the homes of their parents. Never was there known such a viscious devil as this Andilaveris. He used to laugh at everybody, and defied the very Saints in Heaven. On certain days he would take it in the head to climb up to the roof of the Church, and from that height he would drench those who passed underneath with floods of urine, staling away like the Manneken-Pis himself. Before long it was found necessary to adopt more drastic remedies which are generally employed to destroy the vampirish apparitions that are wont to wander abroad at night. Andilaveris was not content then to remain quietly in the grave. Very well, in a little while he would find out to his cost exactly what they were going to do to him. A Friday was chosen as being the only day of the week when the *Broukolakes*, these apparitions, remain in their graves. The village priest, the sexton, and a number of other persons went to the cemetery and opened his tomb. They took the body which was fast asleep, comatose as a snake replete with food, and they bundled it into an old sack which they had brought along with them, putting their horrid burden on the back of a sturdy mule. The little procession took its way to the seaside hamlet of Bryocastro. Immediately all went of board a barque which was awaiting them, and they conveyed their fardel to the tiny islet of Daskaleio. There the priest buried the body in a remote and lonely spot, but this was not done without much difficulty. Andilaveris, who no doubt guessed what was happening to him, awoke from his weekly slumber, and attacked the good priest with vollies of mud and ordure. But in the end they came back home with the satisfaction of knowing that they had freed

their town from the visitations of this foul spectre, for never can a
vrykolakas cross the sea. It is written that only 'the spirit of God moved
over the waters.'"

THE BAJANG

The *bajang* is a species of vampire most dangerous to children.
Supposed to possess the ability to transform itself into a huge cat to
perform its hauntings, the *bajang* is generally believed to be of male sex
and handed down as a bizarre family heirloom. Sir Frank Swettenham
gave the following report of such a demon vampire in 1900:

"Someone in the village falls ill of a complaint the symptoms of
which are unusual; there may be convulsions, unconsciousness, or delirium, possibly for some days together or with intervals between the
attacks. The relatives will call in a native doctor, and at her (she is
usually an ancient female) suggestion, or without it, an impression will
arise that the patient is a victim of a *bajang*. Such an impression quickly
develops into certainty, and any trifle will suggest the owner of the evil
spirit. One method of verifying this suspicion is to wait till the patient
is in a state of delirium, and then to question him or her as to who is
the author of the trouble. This should be done by some independent
person of authority, who is supposed to be able to ascertain the truth. A
further and convincing proof is then to call in a 'Pawang' skilled in
dealing with wizards (in Malay countries they are usually men), and if
he knows his business his power is such that he will place the sorcerer
in one room, and, while he in another scrapes an iron vessel with a
razor, the culprits hair will fall off as though the razor had been applied to his head instead of to the vessel! That is supposing that he is
the culprit; if not, of course he will pass through the ordeal without
damage.

"I have been assured that the shaving process is so efficacious that,
as the vessel represents the head of the person standing his trial, wherever it is scraped the wizard's hair will fall off in a corresponding spot.
It might be supposed that under these circumstances the accursed is
reasonably safe, but this test of guilt is not always applied. What more
commonly happens is that when several cases of unexplained sickness
have occurred in the village, with possibly one or two deaths, the people
of the place lodge a formal complaint against the supposed author of
these ills, and desire that he be punished.

"Before the advent of British influence it—was the practice to kill the wizard or witch whose guilt had been established to Malay satisfaction, and such executions were carried out not many years ago.

"I remember a case in Perak less than ten years ago, when the people of an up-river village accused a man of keeping a *bajang*, and the present Sultan, who was then the principal Malay judge in the State, told them he would severely punish the *bajang* if they would produce it. They went away hardly satisfied, and shortly after made a united representation to the effect that if the person suspected were allowed to remain in their midst they would kill him. Before anything could be done they put him, his family, and effects on a raft and started them down the river. On their arrival at Kuala Kangsar the man was given an isolated hut to live in, but not long afterwards he disappeared."

THE VAMPIRE SHIP

The *Ivan Vasilli*, a Russian steamer built in 1897, was a peculiar setting for vampiric manifestations. In the book *Invisible Horizons*, author Vincent Gaddis related the haunting that began aboard the ship in 1903.

"Its first effects were a sudden feeling that an invisible being was standing nearby. Then came a shock of terror, cold and paralyzing, that drained away all energy like some ghastly suction pump. At times a faintly luminous, misty form, vaguely resembling a human being, could be observed."

The vampiric entity of the *Ivan Vassilli* continued to drain off the vitality of the crew until the ship was a vessel transporting only panic, terror, and death. Three captains, hardened by numerous voyages under the worst conditions, committed suicide. The rest of the crew finally deserted, no longer able to bear the weird and horrifying entity that stalked the decks of the ship.

A crew member named Harry Nelson was the only man to face the vampiric phantom. After extensive observations Nelson reached the conclusion that the creature diminished in perceptibility following each death.

The *Ivan Vassilli* had become a death ship known to be avoided.

Since no one would sail the vessel because of its reputation, the ship was burned in the hope that the vampire would also be destroyed.

CAPTAIN POKROVKSY AND THE VAMPIRE

In 1905, a Russian-Lithuanian Guards officer by the name of Captain Pokrovsky was banished to remain for political reasons at his home in Lithuania. Some time later, however, the government allowed him to visit his uncle for as long as two weeks.

At the beginning of his vacation Captain Pokrovsky accompanied his cousin on visits to the neighbors. While on their walk the girl indicated a man whose vitality seemed to be draining away since his marriage to his second wife. Daily the man became more shriveled while his appetite became insatiable. At night he screamed as if being attacked by some unknown thing.

The captain was perplexed by the situation. Upon asking his cousin the reasons for the pale farmer's condition she said that the villagers believed him the victim of a vampire.

Pokrovsky was thoroughly fascinated by the case. After going through much trouble he succeeded in summoning a doctor from another vicinity to examine the man. The doctor's findings were curious. For the man was dying from loss of blood, although he was not medically anemic, nor were there any substantial wounds about his body. Only a tiny puncture, inflamed at the edges, in his neck indicated any violence. The wound was not swollen as with insect bites. The doctor then gave the man medicines and foods especially fortified for returning his waning strength.

When Captain Pokrovsky's time period ended he was forced by law to return to his estate. The case of the dying man still lingered in his mind. At last he felt compelled to learn the final results, if any, concerning this victim of an unknown parasite.

His cousin informed him that the man had passed away despite the strengthening foods, wines, juices, and medicines. When he died the wound on his neck was noticeably larger. The village was thrown into a state of panic that a vampire was about, with suspicion immediately falling upon the poor man's wife. Even though the woman did not fit any of the traditional descriptions of vampires, and though she devoutly attended church and publicly ate food, she was driven from the district.

Captain Pokrovsky concluded that either the woman was possessed by a vampiric entity or that she somehow attacked her husband while walking in her sleep.

PATINO OF PATMOS

The proceeding account was told to Montague Summers by the Abbott of the Monastery of Amorgos during the former's journey through Greece from 1906-07.

Patino, a merchant from the island of Patmos, went to Natolia on a business trip. There he had the misfortune to die. His wife, hearing of his death, decided it would be most fitting to give Patino a Christian burial in his native soil. Upon her orders the body of Patino was deposited into a coffin and placed aboard a ship bound for Patmos.

During the voyage something uncanny occurred. A sailor, desiring only a moment or two of rest, happened to sit upon the lid of Patino's coffin. To his amazement the occupant of the oblong box seemed to be moving. With a weird expression on his face, the sailor ran to tell the other crew members what had happened. Being a superstitious lot, they believed their comrade, rushed to the coffin, and pulled open the lid. Incredulously they stared at the corpse which was incorrupt and like the body of a living man. Terrified, the sailors nailed shut the coffin in order to keep their promise of safe delivery to the widow.

Deciding to remain silent over the incident, the crew finished the voyage and placed the coffin in the custody of the bereaved wife. With the remains of her husband now in her possession, the woman had them buried in consecrated ground with all the ceremonies of the Church.

But Patino would not remain buried. He began to make forced entries into homes, howling like a wolf and performing acts of violence so that within several days fifteen people had died and the entire area was grasped by panic. There was no doubting that Patino had returned from the grave as a vampire.

The ordained religious of the vicinity attempted to end the vampire's nocturnal prowling through rituals and exorcisms. These unfortunately proved ineffectual in Patino's case. The monks and priests then concluded that the only way to halt the activity of the vampire was to carry his remains back to the place of his death.

The sailors received orders to the contrary. They were instructed to abandon the corpse on the first desert island they encountered, burying it there. Instead of reinterring the body they placed it upon a great pyre and burned it to ashes.

Automatically Patmos was free of further vampire attacks.

Countess Elga

Dr. Franz Hartmann related the following history in an article entitled "An Authenticated Vampire Story," published in the September, 1909 issue of *The Occult Review:*

"On 10 June, 1909, there appeared in a prominent Vienna paper (*The Neues Wiener Journal*) a notice saying that the castle of B— had been burned by the populace, because there was a great mortality among the peasant children, and it was generally believed that this was due to the invasion of a Vampire, supposed to be the last Count B—, who died and acquired the reputation. The castle was situated in a wild and desolate part of the Carpathian Mountains, and was formerly a fortification against the Turks. It was not inhabited, owing to its being believed to be in the possession of ghosts; only a wing of it was used as a dwelling for the caretaker and his wife.

"Now it so happened that, when I read the above notice, I was sitting in a coffee-house at Vienna in company with an old friend of mine who is an experienced occultist and editor of a well-known journal, and who had spent several months in the neighbourhood of the castle. From him I obtained the following account, and it appears that the Vampire in question was probably not the old Count, but his beautiful daughter, the Countess Elga, whose photograph, taken from the original painting, I obtained. My friend said: 'Two years ago I was living in Hermannstadt, and being engaged in engineering a road through the hills, I often came within the vicinity of the old castle, where I made the acquaintance of the old castellan, or caretaker, and his wife, who occupied a part of the wing of the house, almost separate from the main body of the building. They were a quiet old couple and rather reticent in giving information or expressing an opinion in regard to the strange noises which were often heard at night in the deserted halls, or of the apparitions which the Wallachian peasants claimed to have seen when they loitered in the surroundings after dark. All I could gather was that the old Count was a widower and had a beautiful daughter, who was one day killed by a fall from her horse, and that soon after the old man died in some mysterious manner, and the bodies were buried in a solitary graveyard belonging to a neighbouring village. Not long after their death an unusual mortality was noticed among the inhabitants of the village; several children and even some grown people died without any apparent illness; they merely wasted away; and thus a rumour was started that the old Count had become a Vampire after his death. There is no doubt that he was not a saint, as he was addicted to drinking, and some shocking talkes were in circulation about his conduct and that of his daughter; but whether there was any truth in them, I am not in a position to say.

"'Afterwards the property came into the possession of —, a distant relative of the family, who is a young man and officer in a cavalry regiment at Vienna. It appears that the heir enjoyed his life at the capital and did not trouble himself much about the old castle in the wilderness; he did not even come back to look at it, but gave his directions by letter to the janitor, telling him merely to keep things in order and to attend to repairs, in any were necessary. Thus the castellan was actually master of the house, and offered its hospitality to me and my friends.

"'One evening I and my two assistants, Dr. E—,a young lawyer, and Mr. W—, a literary man, went to inspect the premises. First we went to the stables. There were no horses as they had been sold; but what attracted our special attention was an old, queer-fashioned coach with gilded ornaments and bearing the emblems of the family. We then inspected the rooms, passing through some halls and gloomy corridors, such as may be found in any old castle. There was nothing remarkable about the furniture; but in one of the halls there hung in a frame an oil-painting, a portrait, representing a lady with a large hat and wearing a fur coat. We were all involuntarily startled on beholding this picture—not so much on account of the beauty of the lady, but on account of the uncanny expression of her eyes; and Dr. E—, after looking at the picture for a short time, suddenly exclaimed: "How strange. The picture closes its eyes and opens them again, and now it begins to smile."

"'Now Dr. E— is a very sensitive person, and has more than once had some experience in spiritism, and we made up our minds to form a circle for the purpose of investigating this phenomenon. Accordingly, on the same evening we sat around a table in an adjoining room, forming a magnetic chain with our hands. Soon the table began to move and the name *Elga* was spelled. We asked who this *Elga* was, and the answer was rapped out: "The lady whose picture you have seen.

" "Is this lady living?' asked Mr. W—. This question was not answered; but instead it was rapped out: "If W— desires it, I will appear to him bodily to-night at two o'clock." W— consented, and now the table seemed to be endowed with life and manifested a great affection for W—; it rose on two legs and pressed against his breast, as if it intended to embrace him.

"'We inquired of the castellan whom the picture represented; but to our surprise he did not know. He said that it was the copy of a picture painted by the celebrated painter Hans Markart of Vienna, and had been brought by the old Count because its demoniacal look pleased him so much.

"'We left the castle, and W— retired to his room at an inn a half-hour's journey distant from that place. He was of a somewhat sceptical turn of mind, being neither a firm believer in ghosts and apparitions nor ready to deny their possibility. He was not afraid, but anxious to see what would come of his agreement, and for the purpose of keeping himself awake he sat down and began to write an article for a journal.

"'Towards two o'clock he heard steps on the stairs and the door of the hall opened; there was the rustling of a silk dress and the sound of the feet of a lady walking to and fro in the corridor.

"'It may be imagined that he was somewhat startled; but taking courage, he said to himself; "If this is Elga let her come in." Then the door of the room opened and Elga entered. She was most elegantly dressed, and appeared still more youthful than the picture. There was a lounge on the other side of the table where W— was writing, and there she silently posted herself. She did not speak, but her looks and gestures left no doubt in regard to her desires and intentions.

"'Mr. W— resisted the temptation and remained firm. It is not known whether he did so out of principle or timidity or fear. Be this as it may, he kept on writing, looking from time to time at his visitor and silently wishing that she would leave. At last, after an hour, which seemed to him much longer the lady departed in the same manner in which she came.

"'This adventure left W— no peace, and we consequently arranged several sittings at the old castle, where a variety of uncanny phenomena took place. Thus, for instance, once the servant-girl was about to light a fire in the stove, when the door of the apartment opened and Elga stood there. The girl, frightened out of her wits, rushed from the room, tumbling down the stairs in terror with the lamp in her hand, which broke, and came very near to setting her clothes on fire. Lighted lamps and candles went out when brought near the picture, and many other "manifestations" took place which it would be tedious to describe; but the following incident ought not to be omitted.

"'Mr. W— was at that time desirous of obtaining the position as co-editor of a certain journal, and a few days after the above-narrated adventure he received a letter in which a noble lady of high position offered him her patronage for that purpose. The writer requested him to come to a certain place the same evening, where he would meet a gentleman who would give him further particulars. He went, and was met by an unknown stranger, who told him that he was requested by the Countess Elga to invite Mr. W— to a carriage drive, and that she would await him at midnight a certain crossing of two roads, not far from the village. The stranger then suddenly disappeared.

"'Now it seems that Mr. W— had some misgivings about the meeting and drive, and he hired a policeman as detective to go at midnight to the appointed place, to see what would happen. The policeman went and reported next morning that he had seen nothing but the well-known, old-fashioned carriage from the castle, with two black horses, standing there as if waiting for somebody, and that he has had no occasion to interfere, he merely waited until the carriage moved on. When the castellan of the castle was asked, he swore that the carriage had not been out that night, and in fact it could not have been out, as there were no horses to draw it.

"'But that is not all, for on the following day I met a friend who is a great sceptic and disbeliever in ghosts, and always used to laugh at such things. Now, however, he seemed to be very serious and said: "Last night something very strange happened to me. At about one o'clock this morning I returned from a late visit, and as I happened to pass the graveyard of the village, I saw a carriage with guilded ornaments standing in the entrance. I wondered about this taking place at such an unusual hour, and being curious to see what would happen, I waited. Two elegantly dressed ladies issued from the carriage. One of these was very young and pretty, but threw at me a devilish and scornful look as they both passed by and entered the cemetery. There they were met by a well-dressed man, who saluted the ladies and spoke to the younger one, saying 'Why, Miss Elga! Are you returned so soon?' Such a queer feeling came over me that I abruptly left and hurried home."

"'This matter has not been explained; but certain experiments which we subsequently made with the picture of Elga brought out some curious facts.

"'To look at the picture for a certain time caused me to feel a very disagreeable sensation in the region of the solar plexus. I began to dislike the portrait and proposed to destroy it. We held a sitting the adjoining room; the table manifested a great aversion to my presence. It was rapped out that I should leave the circle, and that the picture must not be destroyed. I ordered a Bible to be brought in, and read the beginning of the first chapter of St. John, whereupon the above-mentioned Mr. E— (the medium) and another man present claimed that they saw the picture distorting its face. I turned the frame and pricked the back of the picture with my penknife in different places, and Mr. E—, as well as the other man, felt all the pricks, although they had retired to the corridor.

"'I made the sign of the pentagram over the picture, and again the two gentlemen claimed that the picture was horribly distorting its face.

"'Soon afterwards we were called away and left that country. Of Elga I heard nothing more.'"

A Living Indian Vampire

The incident of a living vampire was recounted in the July 1910 edition of the *Occult Review*.

An English official, one of a small group stationed in the tropics, mysteriously fell ill. Fearing that he would die if he remained there, he applied for a transfer from the Colonial Office. His request was denied and his condition worsened. Unable to cope with the strange malady, he threatened to resign unless he was given the transfer. After finally securing the transfer the official regained his health.

Another official, eighteen months later, complained that upon reaching a certain distance from his bungalow he felt as though a wet blanket was tossed over him, after which he experienced feelings of weakness. As his health degenerated he too was transferred from his post.

A short time after, the once healthy and active wife of the district medical officer fell to the same malady. She was troubled by an external force which made her experience seizures of depression and melancholia. During one of the woman's periods of slumber she screamed and awoke with the story of a monster "having the resemblance of a gigantic spider and huge jellyfish." The husband tried calming her down. But on the next night she was again tormented by the thing. She then revealed that the thing had drained her of so much energy that she could not call her husband for fifteen minutes, during which time she could only lie helpless in bed.

The husband prescribed a vacation, in which the monster in her dreams failed to haunt her. Upon her return, however, she again began to have nightmares, only now of a vampire in human form that bit her neck and sucked out her life.

On a later date the woman passed a man and the street that she seemed to know. To her horror he possessed the features of the vampire in her dreams. She explained the situation to her husband, who ordered that the man be expelled from the vicinity. He was and the dream hauntings never returned.

VAMPIRES OF BULGARIA

In St. Clair and Brophy's *Twelve Years' Study of the Eastern Question in Bulgaria*, 1914, we have an extensive narrative concerning Bulgarian vampires:

"By far the most curious superstition in Bulgaria is that of the Vampire, a tradition which is common to all countries of Slavonic origin, but is now to be found in its original loathsomeness only in these provinces. In Dalmatia and Albania, whence the knowledge of this superstition was first imported into Europe, and which were consequently, though wrongly, considered as its mother-countries, the Vampire has been disfigured by poetical embellishments, and has become a mere theatrical being—tricked out in all the tinsel of modern fancy. The Dalmation youth, who, after confessing himself and receiving Holy Communion as if in preparation for death, plunges a consecrated poniard into the heart of the Vampire slumbering in his tomb; and the supernaturally beautiful Vampire himself, who sucks the life-blood of sleeping maidens, has never been imagined by the people, but fabricated, or at least dressed up, by romancers of the sensational school.

"When that factitious poetry, born from the ashes of a people whose nationality is extinct, and from which civilization has reaped its harvest, replace the harsh, severe, even terrible poetry which is the offspring of the uncultivated courage or fear of a young and vigorous humanity, legendary lore becomes weak, doubtful, and theatrical. Thus, as in a ballad said to be antique, we recognize a forgery by the smoothness of its rhythm; so, when the superstitions of a people naturally uneducated and savaged are distinguished by traits of religion or of sentiment, we trace the defacing hand of the Church or the poet.

"In Dalmatia the Vampire is now no more than a shadow, in which no one believes, or at best in which people pretend to believe; just as a London Scottish volunteer will assure you of his firm faith in the Kelpie and Brounie of Sir Walter Scott, or will endeavor to convince you that he wears a kilt from choice and not for effect. Between the conventional Vampire and the true horror of Slavonic superstition there is as much difference as between the Highland chief who kicked away the ball of snow from under his son's head, reproaching him with southron effiminacy in needing the luxury of a pillow, and the kilted cockney sportsman who shoots down tame deer in an enclosure.

"In Poland the Roman Catholic clergy have laid hold upon this superstition as a means of making war upon the great enemy of the Church, and there the Vampire is merely a corpse possessed by the Evil Spirit, and no longer the true Vampire of the ancient Slavonians. In Bulgaria we find the brute in its original and disgusting form; it is no longer a dead body possessed by a demon, but a soul in revolt against the inevitable principle of corporal death; the Dalmatian poniard, blessed upon the altar, is powerless here, and its substitute is the Ilatch (literally, medicine) administered by the witch, or some other wise woman, who detects a Vampire by the hole in his tombstone or hearth which covers him, and stuffs it up with human excrement (his favourite food) mixed with poisonous herbs.

"We will now give the unadulterated Bulgarian superstitions, merely prefacing that we ought to be well acquainted with it, inasmuch as a servant of ours is the son of a noted Vampire, and is doing penance during this present Lent by neither smoking, nor drinking wine or spirits, in order to expiate the sins of his father and to prevent himself inheriting the propensity.

"When a man who has Vampire blood in his veins—for this condition is not only epidemic and endemic, but hereditary—or who is otherwise predisposed to become a vampire, dies, nine days after his burial he returns to upper earth in an aeriform shape. The presence of the Vampire in this his first condition may be easily discerned in the dark by a succession of sparks like those from a flint and steel; in the light, by a shadow projected upon a wall, and varying in density according to the age of the Vampire in his career. In this stage he is comparatively harmless, and is only able to play the practical jokes of the German Kobold and Gnome, of the Irish Phooka, or the English Puck; he roars in a terrible voice, or amuses himself by calling out the inhabitants of a cottage by the most endearing terms, and then beating them black and blue.

"The father of our servant, Theodore, was a Vampire of this class. One night he seized by the waist (for vampires are capable of exercising considerable force) Kodja Keraz, the Pehlivan, or champion wrestler, or Derekuoi, crying out, 'Now then, old Cherry Tree, see if you can throw me.' The village champion put forth all his strength, but the Vampire was so heavy that Kodja Keraz broke his jaw in throwing the invisible being who was crushing him to death.

"At the time of this occurrence, five years ago, our village was so infested with Vampires that the inhabitants were forced to assemble together in two or three houses, to burn candles all night, and to watch by turns, in order to avoid the assaults of the Obours, who lit up the streets with their sparkles, and of whom the most enterprising threw their shadows on the walls of the room where the peasants were dying of fear; whilst others howled, shrieked, and swore outside the door, even entered the abandoned houses, spat blood 4nto the flour, turned everything topsy-turvy, and smeared the whole place, even the pictures of the saints, with cow-dung. Happily for Derekuoi, Vola's mother, an old lady suspected for a turn for witchcraft, discovered the Batch we have already mentioned, laid the troublesome and troubled spirits, and since then the village has been free from these unpleasant supernatural visitations.

"When the Bulgarian Vampire has finished a forty days' apprenticeship to the realm of shadows, he rises from his tomb in bodily form, and is able to pass himself off as a human being, living honestly and naturally. Thirty years since a stranger arrived in this village, established himself, and married a wife with whom he lived on very good terms, she making but one complaint, that her husband absented himself from the conjugal roof every night (although scavengers were, and are, utterly unknown in Bulgaria) a great deal of scavengers' work was done at night by some unseen being, and that when one branch of this industry was exhausted, the dead horses and buffaloes which lay about the streets were devoured by invisible teeth, much to the prejudice of the village dogs, then the mysterious mouth drained the blood of all cattle that happened to be in any way sickly. These occurrences, and the testimony of the wife, caused the stranger to be suspected of Vampirism; he was examined, found to have only one nostril, and upon this irrefragable evidence was condemned to death. In executing this sentence, our villagers did not think it necessary to send for the priest, to confess themselves, or to take consecrated halters or daggers; they just tied their man hand and foot, led him to a hill outside. Derekuoi, lit a big fire of wait-a-bit thorns, and burned him alive.

"There is yet another method of abolishing a Vampire—that of *bottling* him. There are certain persons who make a profession of this; and their mode of procedure is as follows: The sorcerer, armed with a picture of some saint, lies in ambush until he sees the Vampire pass, when he pursues him with his *Eikon*; the poor Obour takes refuge in a tree or on the roof of a house, but this persecutor follows him up with the talisman, driving him away from all shelter, in the direction of a bottle especially prepared, in which is placed some of the Vampire's favourite food. Having no other resource, he enters this prison, and is immediately fastened down with a cork, on the interior of which is a fragment of the Eikon. The bottle is then thrown into the fire, and the Vampire disappears for ever. This method is curious, as showing the grossly material view of the soul taken by the Bulgarians, who imagining that it is a sort of chemical compound destructible by heat (like sulphuretted hydrogen), in the same manner that they suppose the souls of the dead to have appetites, and to feed after the manner of living beings, 'in the place where they are.'

"To finish the story of the Bulgarian Vampire, we have merely to state that here he does not seem to have that peculiar appetite for human blood which is generally supposed to form his distinguishing and most terrible characteristics, only requiring it when his resources of coarser food are exhausted ... Since commencing this chapter (III), we have learned that the village of Derevishkuoi six hours from here, is just now haunted by a Vampire. He appears with a companion who was suppressed by means of the usual remedy, but this one seems to be proof against poison, and as he will shortly have completed his fortieth day as a shadow, the villagers are in terrible alarm lest he should appear as flesh and blood."

FRITZ HAARMANN, VAMPIRE OF HANOVER

The complete story of Fritz Haarmann, the fiend known as the "Hanover Vampire," appeared under the heading "Vampire's Victims" in the 24 December edition of *The News of the World*.

Fritz Haarmann, born on 24 October 1879, feared and hated his father, a hard-faced locomotive stoker. Unsuccessful in school, young Haarmann joined the service where he was a good soldier. His good took a bad turn when he returned to his home town of Hanover. He was accused of molesting children.

After being placed in a mental institution at Hildesheim, Haarmann broke out and fled to Switzerland. Eventually returning to Hanover, he found himself again quarreling with his father. To escape he enlisted in the 10th Jager Battalion at Colmar in Alsace. Released with a medical discharge, Haarmann again tried to live with his father. The fighting became physical. A Dr. Andrae considered Haarmann completely amoral but could find no legal causes to have him again committed to an asylum.

Taking to the streets, Haarmann survived by theft, fraud, and other crimes, for which he was regularly sent to jail. His release in 1918 placed him as a German cook shop owner. He butchered and sold meat during a time of hunger. Then he changed his profession, working as a spy and police informer for which he earned the nickname "Detective Haarmann."

It was then that Fritz Haarmann began to satisfy his perverse sexual drives. Before dawn he would stroll through the railway station at Hanover, awaken a sleeping young boy, and demand to see his ticket. When a ticket was not produced, Haarmann would hear a sad story after which he would offer the youth a place to stay for the night. Friedel Rothe, seventeen years old and the first to satisfy Haarmann's lusts, was a runaway. Mysteriously Rothe disappeared. The police were on Haarmann's trail, and following a set of clues leading to his home at Cellarstrasse 27 they broke in to find him with another boy in a sexual act violating Section 175 of the German Code, punishable by nine months in prison.

It was not until Haarmann awaited trial for twenty-four killings four years later that he confessed: "At the time when the policemen arrested me the head of the boy Friedel Rothe was hidden under a newspaper behind the oven. Later on, I threw it into the canal."

Haarmann met a handsome twenty-four year-old man named Hans Grans—a blackmailer, male prostitute, thief, spy, informer and murderer—in September of 1919. Grans assumed the job of instigator and organizer in many of Haarmann's murders, including those of Adolf Hannappel, age seventeen, killed November of 1923 when Grans decided he liked the boy's trousers, and Enst Spieker, same age, murdered 5 January 1924 when Grans wanted his shirt. It was a grisly way to get a wardrobe. Together Haarmann and Grans shared a lovers' relationship, Grans becoming the driving force behind Haarmann's murderous desires.

Aside from his experiences with Grans, Haarmann's homosexual acts climaxed in a most peculiar way. Biting into his victim's throat, he satisfied himself by tasting their flowing blood.

In 1924 events occurred to approach putting an end to the vampire career of Fritz Haarmann. Human skulls and bones were found in the Seine River on May 17 and later on the 29th. Two more skulls were dug from a mud bank on June 13. And on July 24, a sack containing more of the same made the police consider the existence of a vampire or werewolf.

Haarmann had been arrested on June 22 on an indecency charge pressed by a boy named Fromm. While Haarmann was in custody, his room in the Red Row was thoroughly searched. Bloodstains were found within the quarters. Although his practice of cutting illegal meat was well known, the vampire and werewolf talk automatically identified the blood as human. The outside evidence was tremendous. Twenty-two corpses, almost all belonging to young men and boys, were discovered. The public was screaming for vengeance against this human monster. Still there was no concrete evidence against Haarmann himself.

At last the mother of one of the missing boys discovered a bit of clothing worn by her son and traced without doubt to Haarmann. The police, weary of the public thinking, questioned Haarmann until he finally confessed and also accused Hans Grans.

Two detailed news stories recounted Haarmann's trial. The first is from a contemporary newspaper:

"Throughout the long ordeal Haarmann was utterly impassive and complacent ... The details of the atrocious crimes for which Haarmann will shortly pay with his life were extremely revolting. All his victims were between 12 and 18 years of ages, and it was proved that accused actually sold the flesh for human consumption. He once made sausages in his kitchen, and, together with the purchaser, cooked and ate them ... Some alienists hold that even then the twenty-four murders cannot possibly exhaust the full toll of Haarmann's atrocious crimes, and estimate the total as high as fifty. With the exception of a few counts, the prisoner made minutely detailed confessions and for days the court listened to his grim narrative of how he cut up the bodies of his victims and disposed of the fragments in various ways. He consistently repudiated the imputation of insanity, but at the same time maintained unhesitatingly that all the murders were committed when he was in a state of trance, and unaware of what he was doing. This contention was specifically brushed aside by the Bench, which in its judgement pointed out that according to his own account of what happened, it was necessary for him to hold down his victims by hand in a peculiar way before it was possible for him to inflict a fatal bite on their throats. Such action necessarily involved some degree of deliberation and conscious purpose."

In the 7 December 1924 edition of *News of the World* the following report appeared:

"The killing of altogether twenty-four young men is laid at his door, the horror of the deeds being magnified by the allegation that he sold to customers for consumption the flesh of those he did not himself eat ... , With Haarmann in the dock appeared a younger man, his friend Hans Grans, first accused of assisting in the actual murders but now charged with inciting to commit them and with receiving stolen property. The police are still hunting for a third man, Charles, also a butcher, who is alleged to have completed the monstrous trio ... the prosecuting attorney has an array of nearly 200 witnesses to prove that all the missing youths were done to death in the same horrible way ... He would take them to his rooms, and after a copious meal would praise the looks of his younger guests. Then he would kill them after the fashion of a vampire. Their clothes he would put up on sale in his shop, and the bodies would be cut up and disposed of with the assistance of Charles."

Finally it was reported: "In open court, however, Haarmann admitted that Grans often used to select his victims for him. More than once, he alleged, Grans beat him for failing to kill 'game' brought in, and Haarmann would keep the corpses in a cupboard until they could be got rid of, and one day the police were actually in his rooms when there was a body awaiting dismemberment. The back of the place abutted on the river, and the bones and skulls were thrown into the water. Some of them were discovered, but their origin was a mystery until a police inspector paid a surprise visit to the prisoner's home to inquire into a dispute between Haarmann and an intended victim who escaped."

Haarmann himself replied when asked how many murders he had committed, "Thirty or forty, I don't remember exactly."

The "Hanover Vampire" was found guilty and sentenced to death, while Grans was imprisoned for life. Haarmann's only comment at the time was, I want to be executed in the market place. On my tombstone must be put the inscription, *Here lies Mass-Murderer Haarmann*. And on my birthday, Hans Grans must come and lay a wreath on it."

Fritz Haarmann was a living vampire. He was executed in traditional fashion. On 15 April 1925 the "Hanover Vampire" was beheaded.

The execution of Fritz Haarmann did not end his case. For it was reported in the April 17 issue of *The Daily Express:* "'*Vampire Brain. Plan to Preserve it for Science.*' Berlin. Thursday, April 16th. The body of Fritz Haarmann, executed yesterday at Hanover for twenty-seven murders, will not be buried until it has been examined at Gottingen University.

"Owing to the exceptional character of the crimes—most of Haarmann's victims were *bitten to death*—the case aroused tremendous interest among German scientists. It is probably that Haarmann's brain will be removed and preserved by the University authorities" —Central News.

Vampires Reported by Ralph Shirley

Recent histories of vampirism in England are few. We have the following narrative by the Honorable Ralph Shirley for the *Occult Review*, Volume XI, Number 5, November, 1924:

"It may be doubted, indeed, in spite of the lack of records, whether vampirism in one form or another is quite as absent from the conditions of modem civilization as is commonly supposed. Although we are not to-day familiar with the Slavonic type of vampire that suck the blood of its victims, producing death in two or three days' time, strange cases come to light occasionally when people are the victims, by their own confession, of something of a similar nature, the vampire in these cases being an entity in human form who indulges in intercourse with someone of the opposite sex. Such cases are to-day, generally speaking, promptly consigned to one of our lunatic asylums and do not reach the public ear. I happened, however, quite recently to hear an instance of the kind. The victim had been engaged to a young man, the family, on account of the man's antecedents, not approving of the engagement, but not being actively hostile. The man died suddenly, and the girl was

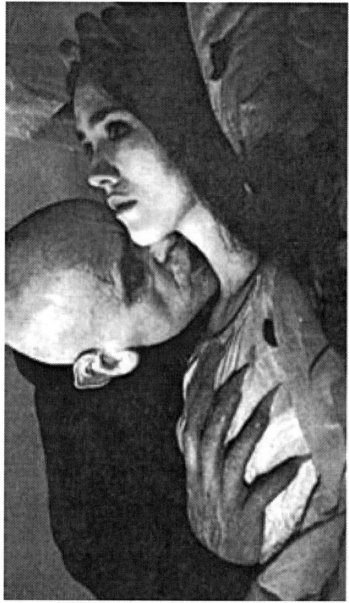

A still from "Nosferatu, Phantom of the Night," a film by Werner Herzog.

prostrated with grief. Shortly after, however, she recovered her normal cheerfulness, and somewhat later confessed to her mother that she was visited by her former lover in physical form. She subsequently became engaged to another man, but owing to threats, as he said, of her deceased lover, the engagement was broken off. The last time I heard of the young lady in question she was stated to be consumptive. Naturally, these things do not get into the papers, and obviously the ordinary medical man will put down instances of the kind as pure hallucination. Still, if we have any belief in the philosophy of the occultist, they are bound to give us pause and make us hesitate before saying that vampirism is entirely a thing of the past."

THE VAMPIRE PRIEST

The vampire is said to cower in the face of religion. The crucifix, the Sacred Host, the words of the Bible make the Undead cringe. But the Church is not without its vampires, as the one reported by R. S. Breene in the *Occult Review*, Volume XLII, Number 4, published in October, 1925:

"The following story was told to me many years ago by persons who were supposed to be relatives of the priest who figures in it. As far as I have been able to find out, I see no reason for doubting that what I am setting down here is approximately a statement of fact. One consideration would have much weight with me in leading me to accept at least the intention of truth in the narrators. The incident happened in a country in Ireland where the vast majority of the inhabitants have always been ardent Roman Catholics. People of this sort would never dream of inventing such a story about an ecclesiastic. So strong is their veneration for the priesthood, and their belief in the sanctity of their parish clergy, that it is almost impossible to understand how such circumstances as I narrate could be associated in the popular mind with the name and memory of one who had received Holy Orders. Yet it was from Roman Catholics who described themselves as eye-witnesses that the information was derived. Again I have read that vampirism only appears in countries which are spiritually in a backward condition, as in some areas of Eastern Europe. Now though, as I have said, the people amidst whom these events took place were Roman Catholics, yet they were not of a high type. The country is wild, isolated and mountainous. Even in recent years numerous terrible crimes of violence have been

reported from the neighbourhood, some of them of a peculiarly sense-
less character. I was myself shown, some years ago, a spot marked with
a white cross upon a stone by the roadside, where a lad of about twenty
years of age had a few nights previously kicked his father's brains out,
of no apparent provocation. One would almost have said, on examin-
ing the evidence in connexion with the case, that there had been something very like demoniac possession. I have never since been in any part
of Ireland where the inhabitants generally seems so conscious of the
interpenetration at all times of the things that are not seen with the
things that do appear. One felt them to be in touch with a realm of
being that we know nothing about in the outer world. They were crude,
brave, and, as we would say, superstitious. The element of fear, the fear
of the unknown, was always to be felt. The most of the inhabitants of
the district were poor, but a number of farmers were able to live in a
certain degree of plain comfort. The publicans and funeral to his
mother's house, which was several miles distant from his parish. It was
from there that the funeral took place. It was a sad picture when the
body came home to the aged mother, whose chief pride in her later
years had been her 'boy in the Church,' the priest; and it was sadder
still when the coffin set out once more from the whitewashed farmhouse, to carry its occupant upon his last journey to the rocky graveyard in the hills where all his kin had laid their bones for generations.
According to custom, all the male and female members of the connexion
accompanied the corpse. The bereaved mother was left to her thoughts
for the rest of the day in the house of death. In the afternoon she
allowed the maid, who did the rough work about the place, to go across
the fields to her own people for a few hours. Mrs.— was as brave as any
other woman of her class, and in her trouble she wished to be alone.

"Meanwhile the funeral cortege wended its slow way (a long procession of traps, jaunting-cars and spring-carts) toward its destination in
the mountains. They did not waste much time in getting their sad task
over and done, but they had a long road to traverse, and the sun was
already declining in the heavens as they climbed the last succession of
hills on the way to the homestead they had left in the morning. It was
a priest's funeral, and, both going and coming, they had not cared to
halt the scattered public-houses they had passed on the wayside, as they
would most certainly have done, and done frequently, in the case of
anybody else's. They were all sober, but many of them, particularly the
womenfolk, had fallen asleep. Night was already in the air. The shadows were lengthening below the hill-crests, but upon the white lime-

stone highway everything was still in broad daylight. At the foot of a
slope the mourners in the first cars suddenly became aware of a solitary
figure coming down towards them walking rapidly. As the distance
between them and the pedestrian lessened they were surprised to see
that he was a priest. They knew of no priest who could be there at such
a time. Those who had taken part in the ceremonies at the grave had
not come so far with them on the return journey. They began to specu-
late as to who the man could be. Remarks were exchanged, and meanwhile the newcomer had met the foremost car. Two men were awake in
it. There could be no mistake. *They saw at once, and quite clearly, that they*
were face to face with the man whom they had laid in his grave two or three
hours before. He passed them with his head slightly averted, but not
sufficiently to prevent them from making absolutely certain of his iden-
tity, or from noting the farmers generally gave one son to the Church.

"A member of the family of M—, a farming connexion, had been
ordained to the priesthood, and was eventually put in charge of a little
hill parish by the local bishop. He is reputed to have been a quiet,
inoffensive man, not given much to the companionship of his flock,
and rather addicted to reading and study. His parishoners listened with
edification to his sermons, brought their children to him for the right
of baptism, made their confession to him at intervals, and took the
sacred bread of the Holy Communion from his hands on Sundays and
the greater festivals of the Church. He did not often conduct stations at

their houses, as did some of his colleagues in other parishes, who were
more gregariously inclined. He was hospitable to strangers, and had
frequently placed beds in his little parochial house at the disposal of
belated travellors and even tramps. Yet no one in his immediate
neighbourhood would have thought of going to see him socially. They
went to him on the Church's business, or they did not go at all. He was,
in a word, respected, though not greatly liked.

"When he had little more than passed his fiftieth birthday, he suddenly fell ill and died, after a brief confinement to his chamber. He was
buried with all the simple pomp that surrounds the obsequies of an
Irish country priest. His body, I should have said, was removed before
the intense, livid palour of his skin, the hard glitter of his wide-open
eyes, *and* the extraordinary length of his strong, white teeth, from which
the full red lips seems to be writhed back till the gums showed themselves. He was wearing, not the grave-clothes in which he had been
attired for his burial, but the decent black frock-coat and garment to

match in which they had last seen him alive. He passed down the long line of vehicles, and finally disappeared round the turn in the road. Some one in every loaded trap or car had seen him; in short, most of those who had been awake and on that side. A thrill of terror passed through the whole party. With hushed voices and blanched teeth they pushed on quickly, not only anxious to get under some sheltering roof and round some blazing hearth before dread night should fall upon them.

"Their first call was at the M— farmhouse. In the front was a little porch built round the door, a small narrow window on either side. About this they gathered, and hurriedly decided to say no word of what had happened to the breaved mother. Then some one knocked, but received no answer. They knocked again, and still being denied admittance, they began to be uneasy. At last some one thought of peeping in through one of the little side-windows, when he saw old Mrs.— lying face downward on the floor. They hesitated no longer, but literally broke in, and it was some little time before they were able to bring her round again to consciousness. This, briefly, is what she told them.

"About half an hour earlier, she had heard footsteps on the flags outside, followed by a loud challenging knock. She was surprised that they should have returned so soon, and, besides, she had been expecting the sound of the cars approaching. She decided that it could not be any of the family, and so, before opening, she looked out at the side. There to her horror she saw her dead son standing in the broad daylight much as she had last seen him alive. He was not looking directly at her. But she, too, noted the extraordinary length of his teeth, the cold blaze of his eyes, I might say the wolfishness of his whole bearing, and the deathly pallor of his skin. Her first instinctive movement was to open the door. Then fear swept over her, swamping even her mother love. She felt her limbs giving way under her, and quickly sank into the oblivion in which she lay until they found her.

"This is the story as it was told to me. If there was a sequel, I never heard it. Was this a case of vampirism? At any rate I have thought it worthy of record."

PETER KURTEN

In appearance Peter Kurten was immaculate, quite uncharacteristic of the monstrous crimes that earned him the titles of "Düsseldorf Vampire" and "Düsseldorf Ripper." His meticulous grooming fit him undetected into the best crowds in a generally uneventful life. It was in the art of shedding blood that Kurten gained his only fame.

Born in 1883 in Mulheim on the Rhine river, Kurten did not like his brutal, drunkard father. He was one of ten children and lived in the same house occupied by the dog catcher. Peter said once that the unclaimed canines were killed and sometimes eaten and that watching the slaughters pleased him. He got pleasure from seeing all types of animals being killed, and from fires and the screams of the people burning.

By the age of nine Peter had committed his first murder. He pushed a young friend off a raft to drown. When a second boy tried to find the youth in the water Kurten made his second killing by pushing him to the same fate. The two deaths filled Peter with a sense of delight and he realized that future killings would give him even more pleasure.

At seventeen Kurten managed to lure an eighteen year-old girl into the woods where he attempted making love to her and strangling her. She escaped, but Kurten harassed her for days afterwards, throwing axes, rocks, firing a gun at her father, and writing letters threatening death if she ever refused his love again. The authorities prevented that threat from becoming reality and Peter spent his next four years in prison.

A year later the sadist was again jailed, this time for seven years. He had been convicted of thirty-four thefts and twelve attempted burglaries. He somehow concealed his four acts of arson. Kurten was released on 13 May 1912, claiming afterwards that he managed to poison two inmates in prison.

Upon regaining his freedom, Kurten resumed his criminal career, including the robbery of an apartment over the café Losch-Ecke. There he found several sleeping children, one a seventeen year-old girl for which he felt a sudden sexual desire to assault violently. He began to strangle her and would have succeeded had he not been forced to run away at the sound of an alarm. A similar attack was foiled when Kurten was discovered but not apprehended in the act of splitting a girl of sixteen with an axe.

Peter Kurten's first murder was committed in the summer of 1913 when, in a house on Wolfstrasse at Düsseldorf, he encountered Christine Klein. The ten year-old girl was sleeping. A strong sexual urge made him go out of control. He clutched the girl around the throat. She struggled then slumped into unconsciousness. Producing a sharp knife from his pocket, Kurten slit her throat, experiencing an orgasm as the blood splashed out. Then the slayer checked his clothing for cleanliness and left the house, returning exhausted to his Düsseldorf apartment. The next day at a café in Mulheim, Kurten found the story of his crime in a newspaper and delighted in the grisly details.

Kurten was convicted of fraud and theft that same year. No one yet realized that he was a killer. Freed in 1921, he married a woman in 1923 who liked his charming ways but did not love him. In her burley way she reminded Kurten of his mother. A convicted murderer herself, she regarded the marriage as yet another form of heavenly punishment for her crime.

In 1929, Peter Kurten began his Jekyll-Hyde career. Externally he was a man of character with a liking for children. Actually he was a psychopathic strangler, slasher, and arsonist. He had a background of seven attempted strangulations and twenty-eight fires, including burning farms, barns, homes, and a forest.

On February 3, seizing a Frau Kuhn and warning her to remain silent, he inflicted twenty four stab wounds on her body. Although still alive when the police arrived, Kurten's method prevented her giving any description of the assailant.

Within five days the mutilated corpse of an eight year-old girl Rose Ohliger was discovered. Stabbed thirteen times, her clothes drenched in kerosene and then burned, the body's discovery infuriated the Düsseldorf populace. Animosity increased even more when the stabbed remains of forty-five year-old Rudolph Scheer was discovered on February 13. Since there was no robbery the criminal had to be a homicidal maniac.

On 2 April 1929, Kurten changed his technique. Erna Pinner, sixteen, was lassoed from behind and yanked off her feet. But Erna was able to fight off the madman and flee, again without seeing the man's face. The following day a similar attempt was made against a Frau Flake but was disrupted by two bystanders. Again no one could describe the attacker.

As the city raged with panic, screaming for a killer, a scapegoat was found in a feebleminded epileptic named Rudolph Strausberg, who confessed to the crimes and was committed to life in a mental institution. Peter Kurten was still at large.

The rippings were resumed on July 30. The mutilated body of Emma

Gross, a prostitute of thirty-four, was found in a run-down hotel. The next day three girls were slashed to near death. Strausberg was obviously not guilty. By the end of August, Kurten had brutally killed nine victims in one month, adding drowning to his methods. In September he added skull—smashing with a hammer to his techniques of choking and cutting. Some of his victims managed to survive, while Düsseldorf achieved the worst reputation imaginable. The unknown killer was so despised that even the criminal world tried to catch and destroy him.

Kurten's murders and attempted killings continued through the end of 1929. At one point he went as far as to inform the *Freikeit*, a Communist newspaper, where the corpse of one Gertrude Albermann would be found.

On May 14 began Kurten's downfall. A young woman, Maria Budlick, arrived at Düsseldorf, which had been quiet since November. Waiting at the railroad station, she was approached by Kurten. Because of his cultured manners, the girl trusted him and agreed to let him find a hotel for her. He was so convincing that Maria stopped at his apartment at 71 Mettmannerstrasse. After eating, Kurten eventually detoured the girl into the Grafenburg woods. As usual he began to strangle her. Then with an almost miraculous change of mind he stopped. Standing back, he asked Maria if she recalled his address. Lying, she said that as a stranger in town she did not remember. He let her go and twenty-four hours later the police were at his door. Maria identified him and he fled down the stairs and out the door. Kurten's wife sickened at her husband's confession and ten days later turned him over to the police. He gave no opposition to the authorities.

Once in custody, after several denials of guilt, he told everything. With utter calmness Peter Kurten revealed that the shedding of blood was a release of sexual tension. He apologized to those victims that survived and admitted that if released he would go back to his bloody way of life. His change in methods had been to confuse the police. Kurten's recounting of his crimes was terribly accurate.

Examined by psychiatrists, Kurten was found responsible for his actions. Each murder was preceded by obvious premeditation. According to German law, on 23 April 1931 he was condemned to die, nine times for every killing. Kurten expressed no self-pity and wished only that people would not hate him. Before his time of execution Kurten wrote apology letters to the survivors of his victims. Astoundingly, he received fan mail, flowers, and marriage proposals from women all over Europe.

Kurten debated with a prison guard as to whether a man might remain alive during a beheading long enough to experience the spilling of his own blood. He learned the answer only minutes later, at 6:00 A. M. on July 2, when Peter Kurten, the "Vampire of Düsseldorf," strode out to the courtyard and submitted his head to the executioner.

This report on Peter Kurten was based on an article written by Bernhardt J. Hurwood.

The Vampire With Red Hair

William Seabrook, in a chapter titled "Vampire 1932 from Brooklyn, N. Y." in his book *Witchcraft, Its Power in the World Today*, related a personal experience with a living, human vampire.

While walking with former *New York Times* journalist Eugene Bagger in the hills behind Le Trayas on the French Riviera, Mr. Seabrook stopped at the latter's house, which at the time was occupied by a variety of persons. Going to the shore for a swim on that hot afternoon, he encountered a girl he already knew. She was of pale complexion, with green eyes and bright red hair. Her name was Mary Lensfield.

Diving from a rock Seabrook cut himself on a stone below the surface of the water. When he returned to shore his shoulder glistened with a streak of fresh blood. At the sight of the blood Mary seemed to go into a trance. Eyes wide open, Mary bit into his shoulder and sucked the blood like a human leech. All the bewildered Seabrook could do was watch.

At that time a truck drove by. The sudden noise snapped Mary from her trance. For a while she and Seabrook sat silently looking at one another. Finally Mary begged to know what was wrong and what to do. Seabrook recalled their first meeting at a party in Brooklyn Heights about two years before when the girl experienced a traumatic event. At the gathering a mystic named Madame Ludovescy claimed to be able to heal wounds supernaturally. She attempted to prove this by using her mouth to stop the bleeding of a sterilized cut in the wrist of host Bob Chandler. Mary became hysterical and fainted. Now Mary was in the same position as Madame Ludovescy. Her mouth was smeared with human blood.

Mary had read and believed much about vampires. She fit certain vampire descriptions, including her flaming hair. The idea that she was a blood-sucking fiend was becoming more than an obsession.

Seabrook attempted to reason with the girl. "Agreed," he said, "you're a 'vampire,' if you insist on calling it that you're a sort of baby vampire who *could* grow up into a monster, but you're not a supernaturally doomed creature, and you're not a criminal either, yet." He recommended she see a psychiatrist.

Mary Lensfield took Seabrook's advice. Within a year, after consulting many specialists in the United States, she died of anemia. Her red blood cells had been disintegrating at a steady rate. By the time her condition was discovered even transfusions would not help.

John George Haigh

John George Haigh was born in to a strict family of the Pilgrim Brethren faith in 1910. The atmosphere of his home bordered on the fanatical. He was not allowed the pleasures of life. It was in such an environment that his vampire personality developed.

Denied friends his own age, young Haigh became obsessed with thoughts of his own salvation. In his mind the only way to attain happiness after death was through the blood of Jesus Christ. If he did not attain salvation, the wrath of an avenging God would lash out at him. His mother was ignorant and superstitious. She implanted in the boy's mind the belief that dreams prophesized the immediate future. Haigh's recurring dreams were of the crucified Christ slowly bleeding to death. (These dreams did affect his future. Whenever Haigh killed he did it quickly so that his victims would not suffer as did Christ.)

In a while Haigh no longer found significance in his family religion. He joined the Church of England, becoming a choir boy and later the assistant organist. One day John claimed to be the recipient of a divine revelation that told him to drink his own urine. Actually this was a bizarre misinterpretation of two biblical passages:

"Drink water out of thine own cistern and running waters out of thine own well." —Proverbs V, verse 15.

"He that believeth on me, as the Scriptures hath said, out of belly shall flow rivers of living water." —John VII, verse 38.

Haigh's dreams of a crucified Christ eventually became that of a forest of crosses which changed into the shapes of trees dripping blood.

As an unknown man collected in a bowl the blood from one tree, it became pale. Haigh in his sleep felt his own body drained of life. The man would then offer the bowl for John to drink, for that was the way to restore his vitality. Each time Haigh reached for the bowl the man faded, drifting back. Awake, unfulfilled, Haigh knew that the only hope of restoration was to drink the blood of human victims.

John George Haigh was a successful vampire. Not until he murdered Mrs. Olivia Helen Henrietta Olive Roberts Durand-Deacon, a widow sixty-nine years of age and his ninth victim, did the police even know of the fiend's existence. He had met the woman in the South Kensington area of London at the Onslow Court Hotel. Luring her to his laboratory on 18 February 1949 to supposedly see his successful experiment in manufacturing artificial fingernails, he shot her through the skull using a .38 Enfield revolver. Then he made an incision in the side of her neck, collected the blood in a drinking glass, and slurped it down. Finally Haigh stripped the corpse naked and dissolved it in a forty-five gallon tank containing thirty gallons of sulphuric acid. The acts were performed without emotion or nausea.

The Kensington vampire made his first mistake when he took his victim's fur coat to the cleaner's and pawned her jewelry. A former friend of the murdered woman, aware of her acquaintance with Haigh, expressed her concern that the widow was missing. She asked Haigh to accompany her to the police station to report the matter. Haigh agreed, but the police detected something wrong with his story. Investigating; the man they learned he had pawned the missing woman's jewelry. Five days later, on February 26, he was taken into custody. After much questioning Haigh admitted his crime plus murders the police did not even suspect. Then he confidently said that he could not be convicted, since there were no bodies to be used for evidence.

The baffled police wondered how to best handle the man. Finally they convinced him to write down an accurate account of his crimes. Haigh wrote down where at Leopold Road to find the sludge remains from the acid baths. A group of Scotland Yard investigators went to the spot and presented their findings to the police laboratory. Police commissioner Sir Harold Scott announced that among the objects discovered were false teeth, the handle of a red purse, three gallstones, pieces of bone, and a yellowish mass of what seemed to be melted fat. The organic materials were undoubtedly human. A dentist furthermore identified the teeth as his own work, made to order for Mrs. Durand-Deacon.

Haigh seemed convicted even before his trial. Although the authorities tried to quiet the matter, several sensational articles concerning the vampire were printed, so that when the court opened at the Sussex Assizes, Lewes, High Street, the building was surrounded by thousands of curious people. Indeed it was an attraction to see an actual living vampire.

During his trial Haigh seemed unaffected by the charges against him. Psychiatrist Dr. Harvey Yellowlees was the only person to testify on his behalf while thirty witnesses spoke against him. As the trial progressed Haigh confessed that his acts were actually religious ceremonies commanded by God, with the consumption of blood necessary for his attaining life forever.

Since the Kensington vampire was fully aware of his crimes, he was found guilty, not insane, and sentenced to be executed. The career of John George Haigh ended when the official hangman's rope broke his neck.

Vampire Corpse
~1952

The discovery of corpses in preserved states have often identified them as being reposing vampires. A French newspaper featured such a story concerning a grave in Italy as late as 1952. The account was related by the French writer Cyrille de Neubourg.

"Blood spurted from a corpse which had been buried since 1920 in the cemetery of Aberici di Montemarciano, in the region of Ancona. The corpse had been exhumed in a perfect state of preservation. The clothes were also in very good condition. It was the corpse of a woman who had died at the age of 70 in February 1920. Blood flowed abundantly from the left knee, and it was only after this outflow that decomposition commenced. No explanation has as yet been found for this phenomenon."

The decomposition after an act of physical mutilation places this case within the traditions of the vampire.

AN ASIAN VAMPIRE

The case of Lem Chee and his vampire wife was published in the book *Strange Monsters and Madmen* by Warren Smith.

In June, 1963, Lem Chee, a wealthy merchant from Hong Kong, began to worry over the condition of his wife. She had been a young and beautiful peasant girl when he met her over twenty years before. Already forty years-old, Lem Chee offered her wealth and love, hoping the differences in their ages would not matter.

At sixty-two, Lem Chee could not help but notice that his wife had not aged.

Fearing that his wife was a vampire, he placed her in a mental institution. There, he reasoned, she would be safe. Once committed to the institution, she tried every means, including escape and bribery of the guards, to get out. None of these attempts proved successful.

The pale-skinned women had been at the institution for six days when she proved her husband's worst fears. She was discovered in the clinic's blood room, drinking down pints of the scarlet liquid. Three quarts of blood were consumed by the woman who claimed she needed it to survive. On another occasion she tried to fasten her teeth to the night nurse's jugular vein.

For the duration of her stay, she was kept away from blood. As a result she aged considerably. She died shortly afterwards, her death being followed a few weeks later by that of her grieving and guilt-ridden husband.

VAMPIRE HUNTER—1970

In August, 1970, *Reuters* told of a twenty-four year-old man named Allan Farrow who was arrested for trespassing in a London graveyard. Farrow, armed with a crucifix and sharpened wooden stake, was caught by police at St. Michael's Churchyard. He said that he was on his way to Highgate Cemetery, where a vampire was supposedly hiding.

"I decided to visit it and see if I could find the vampire and destroy it," said Farrow. "Had the police not arrived it was my intention to make my way to the gravestones and the catacombs in search of the vampire."

Artist Edvard Munch's painting, "The Vampire."

BIBLIOGRAPHY

Heiman, Leo. "Meet the Real Count Dracula." *Fate*. Vol. 21-No. 3 (March, 1968), 53-60.

Hill, Douglas, and Pat Williams. *The Supernatural*. London: Aldus Books, 1965.

Hurwood, Bernhardt J. *Monsters and Nightmares*. New York: Belmont Productions, 1967.

—*Monsters Galore*. New York: Fawcett Publications, 1965

—*Terror by Night*. New York: Lancer Books, 1963.

—*Vampires, Werewolves, and Ghouls*. New York: Ace Books, 1968.

Rogo, D. Scott. "Reviewing the Vampire of Croglin Grange." *Fate*. Vol. 21-No. 6 (June, 1968), 44-48.

—"In-Depth Analysis of the Vampire Legend." *Fate*. Vol. 21-No. 9 (September, 1968), 70-77.

Seabrook, William. *Witchcraft: Its Power in the World Today*. New York: Harcourt, Brace & Co., 1940.

Smith, Warrne. *Strange Monsters and Madmen*. New York: Popular Library, 1969.

Spence, Lewis. *Encyclopedia of Occultism*. New Hyde Park: University Books, 1960.

Stoker, Bram. *Dracula*. London: Constable, 1897.

Summers, Montague. *The Vampire: his Kith and Kin*. London: Routledge and Kegan Paul, 1928. New Hyde Park: University Books, 1960.

—*The Vampire in Europe*. London: Routledge and Kegan Paul, 1929. New Hyde Park: University Books, 1962.

—*The Werewolf*. London: Routledge and Kegan Paul. New Hyde Park: University Books, 1966.

Volta, Ornella. *The Vampire*. France: Editions Jean Jacques Pauvert. Translated by Raymond Rudorff, London: Tandem Books, 1965.

Wright, Dudley. *Vampires and Vampirism*. London: William Rider and Son, 1914.

SENSE OF WONDER PRESS 2004 Catalogue

ACKERMANTHOLOGY
Compiled by Forrest J Ackerman
Introduction by John Landis
6x9, 308 pages
Trade Paper   0-918736-25-0 $19.95
Trade Cloth   0-918736-59-5 $34.95

ANARQUÍA
An Alternate History of the Spanish Civil War
by Brad Linaweaver and J. Kent Hastings
Just nominated for "Prometheus Award for Best Novel"
6x9, 237 pages, Illustrated
Trade Paper   0-918736-33-1 $21.95
Trade Cloth   0-918736-50-1 $35.95

CLAIMED
by Francis Stevens
Selected by Forrest J Ackerman
*"One of the strangest and most compelling science fantasy
novels you will ever read."* —H.P. Lovecraft
6x9, 192 pages, Illustrated
Trade Paper   0-918736-37-4 $15.95
Trade Cloth   0-918736-57-9 $27.95

DR. ACULA'S THRILLING TALES OF THE UNCANNY
Compiled by Forrest J Ackerman, 6x9, 265 pages, Illustrated
Trade Paper   0-918736-30-7 $19.95
Trade Cloth   0-918736-61-7 $34.95

Expanded Science Fiction Worlds of FORREST J ACKERMAN & FRIENDS PLUS
By Forrest J Ackerman with 7 new collaborations
6x9, 205 pages, Illustrated
Trade Paper   0-918736-26-9 $17.95
Trade Cloth   0-918736-58-7 $28.95

FAMOUS FORRY FOTOS
Kodakerman Memories by Forrest J Ackerman
6x9, 117 pages, Photos
Trade Paper   0-918736-32-3 $14.95
Trade Cloth   0-918736-56-0 $34.95

LON OF 1000 FACES!
by Forrest J Ackerman
8.5x11, 300 pages, Illustrations, 1000+ Photos
Trade Paper   0-918736-39-0 $29.95
Trade Cloth   0-918736-53-6 $54.95

THE MAGIC BALL FROM MARS and STARBOY
By Carl L. Biemiller, Introduction by Anne Hardin
6x9, 302 pages, Illustrated, Ages 7-12
Trade Paper   0-918736-09-9 $19.95
Trade Cloth   0-918736-10-2 $38.95

MARTIANTHOLOGY
Compiled by Forrest J Ackerman
Edited by Anne Hardin
6x9, 266 pages, Illustrated
Trade Paper   0-918736-45-5 $19.95
Trade Cloth   0-918736-46-3 $34.95

METROPOLIS
Novel by Thea von Harbou with "Stillustrations" from
Fritz Lang*s film by the same title.
8.5x11, 262 pages, Illustrated
Trade Paper   0-918736-35-8 $23.95
Trade Cloth   0-918736-54-4 $45.95
Ltd. Edition   0-918736-34-X $60.00

RAINBOW FANTASIA
35 Spectrumatic Tales of Wonder
Selected by Forrest J Ackerman
Introduction by Anne Hardin
6x9, 562 pages, Illustrated
Trade Paper   0-918736-36-6 $29.95
Trade Cloth   0-918736-60-9 $44.95

TRUE VAMPIRES OF HISTORY
by Donald F. Glut
6x9, 132 pages, Illustrated
Trade Paper   0-918736-67-6 $14.95
Trade Cloth   0-918736-68-4 $23.95

TRUE WEREWOLVES OF HISTORY
by Donald F. Glut, Illustrated
6x9, 136 pages, Illustrated
Trade Paper   0-918736-69-2 $14.95
Trade Cloth   0-918736-70-6 $23.95

WOMANTHOLOGY
Compiled & edited by
Forrest J Ackerman and Pam Keesey
6x9, 363 pages, Illustrated
Trade Paper   0-918736-33-1 $21.95
Trade Cloth   0-918736-50-1 $35.95

Complete Story/Author lists for all Ackermanthologies at:

http:\\www.senseofwonderpress.com

Order from all major bookstores including amazon.com,
barnesandnoble.com or directly from Sense of Wonder Press
through our secure shopping cart.

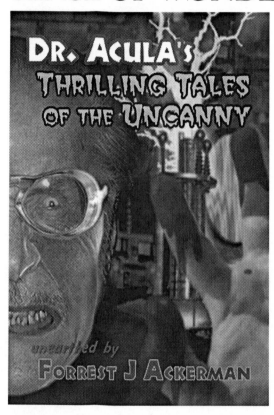

CPSIA information can be obtained at www.ICGtesting.com
Printed in the USA
LVOW12s2130080115

422100LV00002B/278/P

9 780918 736673